Grief & Recovery

STANDING *in the* FIRE

a companion book for
facing the loss of a loved one
and life without them

Diana E. Percy

Copyright © 2020 by Diana Percy

Cover Design by Kim Percy

Internal Design and typesetting by Kim Percy, Designscope

Author profile illustration by Jess Coppet

First published 2020 by Di Percy Family Trust

ISBN 978-1-922357-13-7 (paperback)

ISBN 978-1-922357-14-4 (ebook)

All rights reserved. No part of this publication may be reproduced, distributed, or transmitted in any form or by any means, including photocopying, recording, or other electronic or mechanical methods, without the prior written permission of the publisher, except in the case of brief quotations embodied in critical reviews and certain other non-commercial uses permitted by copyright law. The publisher can be contacted at info@dipercy.com

Please Note: The ideas and suggestions contained in this book are intended for your growth and wellbeing and are not intended as a substitute for individual medical or psychological advice from your health care professional. The reader is advised and encouraged to seek the aid of a qualified healthcare practitioner for advice pertaining to his or her particular need and conditions.

Testimonials

"Standing in the Fire is a beautiful book that inspires hope and meaning for living and dying, with healing words for the losses life brings us especially from mid-life on. This is the book to hold as a fellow grief traveller. It is a wise friend, mindful mentor, loving healer and artful commentator.

Di Percy bridges psychological insight and practical application. Grief is inevitable in life, and this book will be your perfect companion before, during and after that time."

—Chip Conley
The Modern Elder Academy; New York Times bestselling author; entrepreneur Air BnB and Joi de Vivre.

"Thank you, Di Percy, for being willing to share your experiences and for finding a language for us all to talk about death and dying and about how our lives can be enriched when we become a Dying Companion."

—Professor Mary Foley, AM
former Director General and Secretary of NSW Health, Australia

"A healing and insightful book of living in the presence of dying, with stories and commentary of grief and recovery told gently without shying from suffering. Standing in the Fire is an act of kindness befitting loved-ones and professional caregivers."

—Dr Francis Macnab, AM, OM
Professor Emeritus; Founder Cairnmillar Insitiute of Psychotherapy

"Standing in the Fire is a work of metaphor and practicality, spiritualism and worldliness, shadow and light. It is like a wise friend accompanying you through loss, grief and recovery and a book to keep close, to help us feel comfort and make meaning of it all.

Diana Percy has written this book like going on a sacred pilgrimage, becoming immersed in our process and arriving at the end restored."

—Justine Willis Toms
Host, New Dimensions Radio USA, author of *Small Pleasures: Finding Grace in a Chaotic World*

"Standing in the Fire made me feel seen and understood in where I am with my mother as her dying companion— consoled and inspired and then left full of hope and curiosity."

—Mari O'Connell
Carer and Soul Companion, Ireland

"Standing in the Fire is an insightful, wise and intimate travel companion in our journey with grief, healing, ritual, hope and renewal. When our world is dark, our hearts leaden and grief immobilises us, this is the book that encourages us to explore different paths of healing in a spirit of gentle compassion, learning and inner peace.

Diana offers the hand of companionship to explore new growth and possibilities that emerge from our darkest days. A timely, wise and courageous book that offers us the opportunity to think differently about the light as well as the shadow of grief."

—Nora Vitens
Creator, Viva 70 Lifestyle Magazine on Ageing Well

Acknowledgements

I wish to thank: my family for their love and support during and after the dying time; my neighbours who are the salt of the earth and I miss dearly. Dr Cath Crock for her trust in the book and being a visionary of truth, goodness and the arts; Yamini Nadu and Carolyn Tate for their encouragement and friendship and together with Kath Walter's abounding know-how, we formed the best writers group ever; Mari O'Connell and Jacqui Cooper, my generous and wise first readers; Lu Sexton; Ben and Michelle Phillips for their support and editorial care; Kim Percy for her patience, love, stunning design, and going the extra mile; and Zaya and Maurizio Benazzo who lovingly created and tilled the fertile ground of Science and NonDuality Italy, in which this book first grew from the original seed.

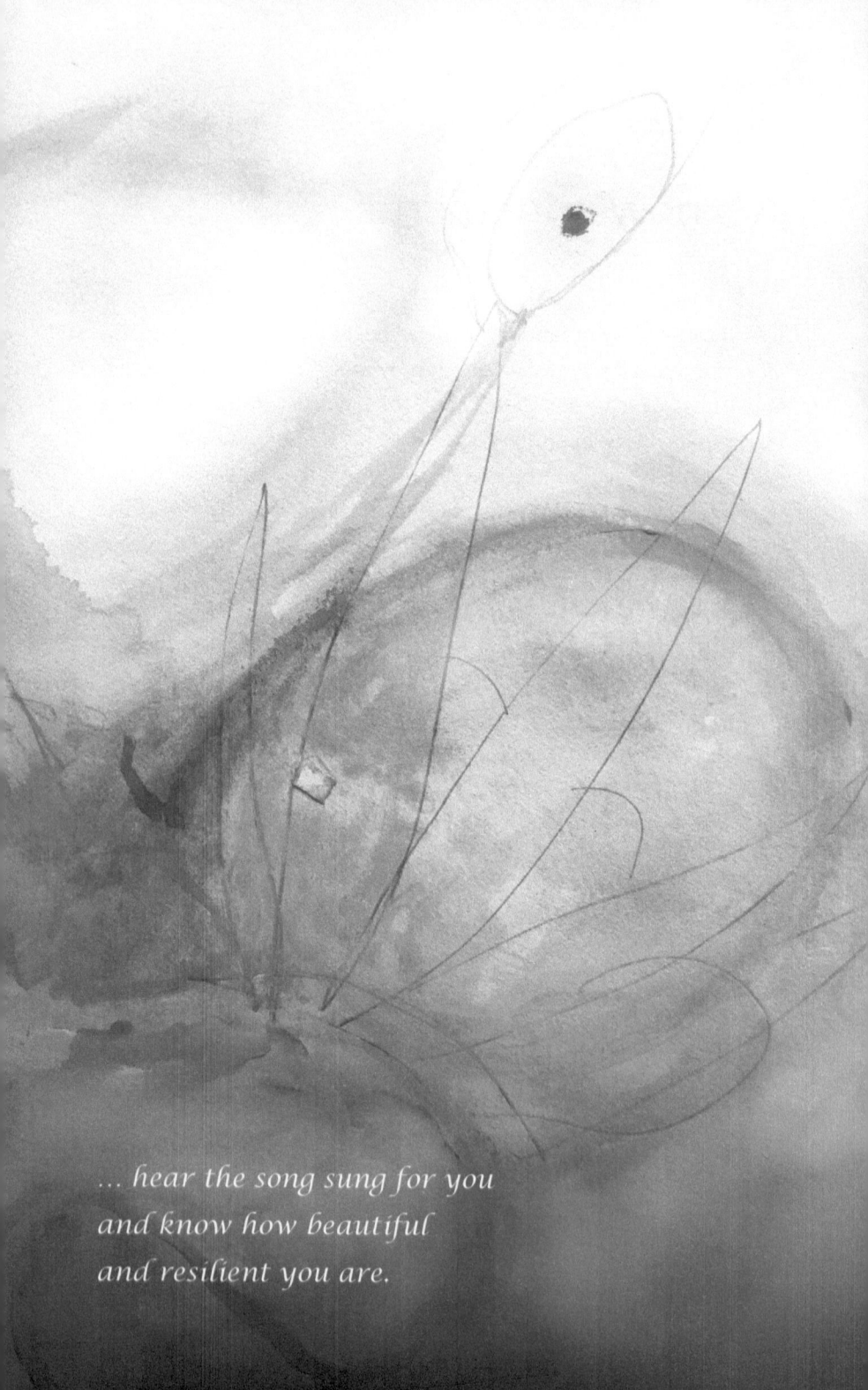

Contents

FOREWORD Dr Catherine Crock — iii
PROLOGUE Maurizio Benazzo — vi

INTRODUCTION — 15
A Fire that Heals; The Thresholds — 22

I. Facing Terrible Uncertainty
The First Threshold: Fire — 27

1. Will Your Loved-One Live or Die — 29
2. Becoming a Dying Companion — 39
3. Gone: The Loss of Your Loved-One — 60
4. Rites of Passage — 73

II. Grieving as Sacred Process
The Second Threshold: Pilgrimage — 83

5. The Person is Gone: Your Relationship Continues — 88
6. Soulwork — 100
7. Loneliness and Solitude — 118
8. Grieving as Sacred Process — 137
9. Mystics and Spiritual Teachers on Death — 144
10. A Pilgrim's Journal Extracts — 157

III. Living Without Them
The Third Threshold: Beauty — 173

11. Seeing Beauty — 175
12. Healing, an Ancient Art — 181
13. Wise Life Guides — 193
14. Return to the Community — 202
15. Silken Threads — 213

IV. Ritual and Contemplation — 223
List of Practices and Thoughts: Healing — 231

Bibliography — 264
Meet the Author — 266

Foreword

This vitally important book fills a gap between the healthcare system being focussed on care for the dying, and what happens to you as the companion during the process and afterward. Often there is not the time or resources for support and learning for the companion. Standing in the Fire is the resource to help you understand what you are going through and guide you on this journey yourself. The book gently accompanies loved-ones and family through grief and recovery.

When Di Percy and I first spoke about this book, the synergies were clear. The Hush Foundation is dedicated to incorporating the arts as the means of advancing a patient-centred healthcare culture. In her creativity and sensitive treatment of the personal experience of grief, Di has written a book that stands alongside all our artists and musicians.

Kindness is at the centre of Standing in the Fire. It is an integral theme demonstrated time and again for the one dying and in particular for the loved-one and personal carer left behind. Professional carers can be deeply affected too by the loss of their patient, and this book is as much for them with words to help heal the healers.

Kindness is such a powerful force, as both a value and a practice. It is a force that can transform experience from one of fear to one of support for those dying, their families and loved ones. Kindness can positively transform the experience and culture of health professionals as well, and for many years I have been advocating for kindness to be at the centre of our healthcare system.

The growing need for more support of the loved-ones, families and carers of those dying is undeniable. This book provides an easily accessible and private support that can be taken with you, to be read at anytime, anywhere. Just reading a phrase or two at the right time can make the difference between being weighed down or more resilient that day.

Throughout the book, Di explores different ways to make meaning out of grief and loss, expanding the idea that with meaning, grief becomes bearable, and recovery brings hope.

The first three parts of the book represent three stages of loss and grief: facing the ending, the grieving process, and living life without them. Part four is the practical part of the book describing how to conduct over 30 different rituals, contemplations and practices to assist these stages of grief and recovery.

Di has a deep understanding of death and dying through personal experiences of the loss of loved-ones, of counselling those dying and the ones grieving their loss. She held a professional position as the trainer and clinical supervisor of 200 counsellors dealing with crisis, loss and bereavement.

As a leader in this area, she stands to make a difference through her words, weaving kindness, hope and courage throughout the pages.

This book is an inspiring investigation into how to nurture ourselves in the midst of grief and recovery, then to contemplate living a fulfilling and meaningful life, without the one we love.

Professor Catherine Crock, AM
Faculty of Health, Deakin University;
Physician, Royal Children's Hospital, Melbourne;
Chair and Founder of the Hush Foundation;
Founder of the Australian Institute for Patient and Family Centred Care.

Prologue

The relationship to our mortality, how we approach the mystery of death, has a huge impact on how we approach and navigate life.

In this beautiful and creative book, Diana Percy expresses the tradition of Nonduality, and in its pages we see living and dying not as polarities, but as a continuous cycle. She takes us by the hand with kindness, and walks with us through the many pathways of grief and loss until we reach a place in which we are seeing beauty.

Then, and only then, we can lay to rest by having known shadow and light, grief and love and, at last, recognising and appreciating our own life.

Maurizio Benazzo
Co-founder, Science and Nonduality
www.scienceandnonduality.com

Introduction

A Fire that Heals

Standing in the fire best described the way my grief felt, a burning ache inside for all that was and all that had not been. It was a profoundly personal experience. The journey with my dying loved-one was brutal and heartfelt, and I would not have missed it. It was where I was meant to be. Everything going on in my life was dropped to be there with him over the last months.

Walking toward death with someone you love is the darkest and saddest time of life. It is also an immense privilege. There is no need to worry about how you will get through it because your body-soul, in its innate intelligence, will lead the way. Grief does that. It embodies and takes over so completely that we have to go with it. There is no choice, except resistance, refusal. In the end that harms.

The overwhelm and ache of "standing in the fire" eventually ran its course. As the fire eased, having done its work, I was left in a super-receptive state. This is the time we can open our mind to seeing beauty the most powerful healing force that I know. What happens between the intensity of fire and the lens of beauty, is a sacred inner pilgrimage of grief, and the time we start to make meaning.

Three parts of the book reflect three phases of loss and grief: uncertainty and ending, the grieving process, and living without them. Each phase is represented by a symbolic threshold: Fire symbolises Terrible Uncertainty and Endings; Pilgrimage symbolises Grieving as Sacred Process; and Beauty symbolises Living Life Without Them. Each threshold is where we gather our selves, prepare and find meaning until ready to step through and beyond the threshold to what is next. Part IV of the book, Ritual and Contemplation, assists with healing practices for each threshold.

I. Facing Terrible Uncertainty and Ending
The First Threshold: *Fire*

Not knowing whether your loved-one will live or die can be just as agonising as knowing for certain they will die. The first threshold explores the experience and stages of Facing Terrible Uncertainty and Ending. Personal experiences of others who have faced the death of their loved-one are shared. I walk with you through the dying process, and finally your actual loss.

Going through the dying process with someone you love is not often talked about. Mostly, the focus is on the dying person. Yet the experience is intense for both of you and the focus here is more on you as the one left behind. We never know for sure that death is certain nor when it will occur, but the words on each page aim to be your companion through the stages of uncertainty and loss. It is a distressing time and I held you in my mind as I wrote.

II. Grieving as Sacred Process
The Second Threshold: *Pilgrimage*

Regarding grief as a sacred process elevates grieving from an ordeal of suffering to a privileged expression of love. A pilgrimage is a sacred process, with the pilgrim embarking on an inner journey as they pass through unfamiliar lands. Travelling through grief is an inner pilgrimage, with memories and reflections about where we have come from with our loved-one, where we are now, and where we will go.

Grief is compounded when we become anxious or afraid, or think our experience is not normal. For that reason, stories, journal entries and perceptions of grieving are shared. Spiritual teachers outline wisdom of ways to approach death and grieving. Loneliness and the fear of loneliness can become a concerning and consuming experience. The healing ways of Soulwork are introduced and outlined, such as learning from difficult emotions and turning loneliness to solitude.

III. Living Life Without Them
The Third Threshold: *Beauty*

There comes a time that you are ready to go on in life without your loved-one, to readjust your experience of walking the earth without their physical touch and presence. Readiness to do so comes gradually. We are not the only ones, and through our own suffering may better understand the suffering of others, and hold the torch of hope and healing for them.

The third threshold is all about readiness and renewal. It outlines an active and powerful practice of seeing beauty to support your path and recover your place in the world. You may see your community with fresh eyes and realise you are not alone, that many grieve and suffer. Ralph Waldo Emerson put it so clearly: "To leave the world a bit better, whether by a healthy child, a garden patch, or redeemed social condition; to know even one life has breathed easier because you live—that is to have succeeded." We look beyond bereavement to our path as life pilgrims and the task that now exists for our own life.

IV. Ritual and Contemplation
List of Practices: *Healing*

Rituals are symbolic ceremonies of meaning and structure, in our case to assist with grieving. Rituals are suggested throughout the book and Practices to aid healing are described in Part IV. The practices are designed to be applied and comforting. You will find ways to shift your attention from one place to another place without indulging or denying the grief that we go through, the standing in the fire that paradoxically purifies and mends heartache. The symbolic actions of ritual provide an intervening structure of meaning.

Contemplation is to consider deeply on sacred ground and in the temple of our mind-body, to find what has been hidden or obscure. There is a touch of awe and wonder about this. Some guided meditations are outlined for you including walking meditations (instruction for "Little Pilgrimages" are on my website). Contemplation could be reading a poem or book section and taking time to reflect on what its message is for you.

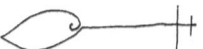

Death and dying are not freely talked about in our society, so grieving is often a long, lonely experience. I have written the book so you may not feel so alone and can pick it up to read anytime, whatever part of grief and loss you are now going through.

Standing in the Fire is a companion book for facing the loss of a loved-one and life without them. The words are heartfelt, born of my losses, of being a companion to my husband and other loved-ones while dying, and the privilege of counselling those left behind. Standing in the Fire rests on a lifelong immersion in poets, spiritual teachers and mystics who have so much to teach us about living and dying. Many people are afraid of death and dying—we are afraid of emotional suffering, of sorrow, and the unknown beyond life. Facing the death of someone we care about is an intensely personal experience and at the same time a shared universal experience. Fears can be dissolved.

Grief, like fire, is a living force. Grief shares the qualities of fire, from the flame of love to the burning of pain. Grief can flare up out of the blue without any regard for time or place, and, sometimes without warning, warm our heart by bathing it in love. Although it feels like it will never end, grief ultimately burns itself out and we are left wiser and kinder in its embers.

Fire and Metaphor

This a book of hope, courage, wonder and investigation. The subject of dying and grieving lends itself to metaphor. It is essentially a companion book for your personal path, not an instructional "how-to" book. Fire is universally considered a spiritual symbol of transformation and awakening. Fire can be constructive or destructive, depending on whose hands it is in. Standing in the fire of grief is transformational when it is not blocked or pushed down and is left to run its natural course.

Sacred and ancient texts, such as the I Ching, the Buddhist Sutras, the Bible, Koran and Torah, name fire as a purifying energy. These sacred texts speak about the fire of the soul; the fire of the heart; the fire of vision; the fire of learning; and the creative fire. These five timeless representations of fire symbolise universal human experience and yearning for meaning, deepening and transcendence.

Fire is rich in symbolism, even symbolising polarities and opposing forces. We can say fire is unity in opposites—life and death, destruction and creativity, apocalypse and illumination, suffering and transcendence. We can question whether these polarities are opposites, or pairs needing synergy. Fire symbolises both anger and the beautiful flame of love, and grief teaches us about polarities we may hold within.

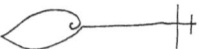

It is now two years since my husband died. Throughout the book I share with you my grieving experiences in stories, journal entries, poetry and commentary. There are also true stories of people told in my words, with names changed for their privacy. Conversations with the one dying have led to the conclusion that, as in living, dying is about "doing it my way". There is no right way or good death and letting go of a sense of failure makes dying peaceful, so death can come with a feeling of having completed life, perfect in its imperfection, and with love for those close.

Primarily, the book is written for the one left behind, someone you love: your life partner, close friend, your child, your own parent or loved family member. I hope that reading *Standing in the Fire* brings you comfort and companionship. I hope it stirs your courage, hope and love. In your own way and the ways that bring you joy, I hope it stirs you to give something of yourself to make a better world.

An Approach to Death and Loss

For reasons I don't fully understand, humans have come to me when they are dying. Death has been part of my life from childhood onward, starting with an aunt we lived with, followed by my father's death when I was eight years old after he had been ill and dying for all of my young life. While I was in my twenties, other close family members died and they called me to have a part in their dying time. After that two young men forever stand out, independent of each other, one a friend and the other a client. Tragically they were both dying although they had everything to live for. One helplessly mourned his life slipping away from him over two years and died from cancer at twenty-nine years old. The other was a husband and father of three little children. He endured four long years of fearsome operations and treatment on a brain tumour that slowly took away his mobility before it took his life. His mischievous sense of humour initially brought him courage as he desperately fought to live. But it was not to be. Both young men sought me for support and counselling, gripped with fear, waves of anger and deep despair. I understood that apart from a planned death, nature is totally indiscriminate and none of us have any say in when we die.

Consequently, death contributed to shaping my approach to life. Mostly I have tried to live as though this year, this day, could be my last, which led me to be too much the daredevil in my younger years but has become wise counsel as I age. Death has been a teacher, a constant reminder that my end may not be far away. We just don't know. That thought has always been a motivator for me—I had better get on with it and do what I came here to do.

The Thresholds

At the most significant times of life, when we take pause to reflect and gather our selves, we find potential for great meaning. What does not matter anymore becomes evident, and what we truly value rings clear and comes sharply into focus. Slowly but surely we become aware that on the path in front there lies a threshold. We cannot go back to where we were before arriving here, for to do so would be to lose our soul—although without a helping hand sometimes that option is taken. Soul loss is a detachment from what is meaningful and life-generating. Contemplating this position, though, the realisation is inescapable: there is no other way but onward and through.

You know you are at the threshold when you feel or sense that you have turned a corner. Everything has changed. There is no control over any of it. Being at the threshold is to be in a liminal state, that is a state of transition. By external standards we may be standing still, but internally we are in dynamic transition as we prepare mind, body and spirit for the future. Instinctively, we know it as a time of significance, that life is undergoing a seismic readjustment from the inside out.

Three thresholds of grief together map the metaphorical gateways in an otherwise long and bleak landscape of dying and loss. The thresholds are rest points and markers to help find the way and make our path through the grieving landscape.

The pilgrim is the one travelling an inner passage of grieving, this is the long, solo work of grief. The inner pilgrimage affects us deeply and takes us to the work of the soul, outlined in the chapter on Soulwork, that enables us to see beauty and return to the community.

Initiations

Each threshold is a time of initiation. It takes time to prepare to go through the threshold and be ready for what lies on the other side. The task at each threshold reminds us of our many inner resources, and to be hopeful, take courage and perfect our love (not the self) as we move forward. There are many insights to uncover as we reflect on all it has taken to get here and the way we went about it.

The threshold initiations prepare us to let go of the life we had with our loved-one and move on to the next part of life. Buddhist teacher, Jack Kornfield, has found that "Initiation offers a test to abandon the old and open to a greater vision". There are unknowns yet to unfold. One way or another, we move on regardless. The rewards are not only for our selves but also what we bring to others and accordingly, the way we will live the rest of our life.

It may seem we lose everything with our loved-one gone, yet grief can nurture the growth of meaning and wisdom. We can take inspiration from Viktor Frankl as he was initiated time and again to loss and grief in the most brutal ways, and said everything can be taken from us except, "… the last of human freedoms—to choose one's own attitude in any given set of circumstances, is to choose one's own way."

We can choose the way of self-knowledge and to be available for others in their grief and suffering. Could it be that suffering brings forward the world's love and grace through each of us?

I | Facing Terrible Uncertainty and Ending

The First Threshold: *Fire*

The task at the First Threshold of Fire is to face terrible uncertainty, impending loss, and the pain of the ending. Everyone will come to this threshold sooner or later where for many, pain and dread threaten to envelop like a fire within. It is undoubtably the most daunting of the three thresholds. Yet staying right there at the Fire threshold, without trying to rush away, surprisingly becomes healing. The fire of grief will die down partly of its own accord and partly by dousing the flames with tears. The time comes soon enough to pass through this threshold and go on to the next.

This fiery threshold urges us to face the sorrow of being with one dying, then to stand right in the fire of grief when they are gone, knowing our painful emotions are not to be feared. Grieving emotions are natural, there to be experienced rather than pushed down. Fire is transformational and the intensity of grief will recede given time, then transform, and ultimately heal and warm.

You and your loved-one share being at this same threshold, although it is a different experience for each of you. Your loved-one is dying and in transition toward death. You are with them in their transition and in a spiritual sense, you are also their compassionate witness. At the same time, it is the start of your transition to their ending and the end of your life together.

When someone is dying, we can get carried along by the practicalities and tasks of the moment—dealing with all the medical, legal and functional tasks that suddenly come up; coming to terms with pieces of medical information as it gets delivered, often drip by drip; thinking about necessities that must be done; and caring for other mourners in their impending loss. These things need to be dealt with but they can dominate our thinking, taking us away from simply being present with our loved-one.

Are they going to die? The question circles around. It can be a long wait for clarity. Some get the terrible and unwanted clarity early on: the illness is terminal. Or your loved-one was in an accident and it is only a matter of time. Whatever way it happens, being at the threshold of fire is a heart-wrenching in-between state. Life is no longer what it was and you are yet to find out what it will become.

The task at this threshold is big. Friends and counsellors can do only so much. We must give it time and summon our vast and untapped inner resources. You are more courageous and more resourceful than you know. We all are.

Chapter 1

Will Your Loved-One Live or Die

The first inkling that a loved-one might die seems impossible, unsurmountable. This is especially so if they are still young, or at least nowhere near old enough to die in your eyes. As time passes, slowly it starts to become likely or inevitable that they might be dying. As we confront our worst fears, it's a struggle to keep them at bay. It can feel unbearable. When that happens, it is as though life has turned upside down. We are in unfamiliar territory waiting for some certainty, hoping and praying the moment of truth will be that they are going to pull through.

We were in shock the first time my husband and I had a conversation with the doctor that started with those shattering words, "This is bad news, I'm afraid". After the consultation, we went to the hospital cafe for coffee and called a good friend hoping that telling him about it would somehow lessen the blow. "Martin has three cysts in his pancreas. The operation is scheduled for next week." But our friend was busy and failed to recognise the dire significance of this, so we were left to our own resources. We didn't want to call family until what it all meant had been grasped more fully, and besides we needed more information—more certainty. "It is probable the cysts are malignant", the doctor said. Probable? But not certain. Everything seemed up in the air. We didn't want to distress the kids unnecessarily (they are all adults). So in our bewilderment, driving home to the farm from the city hospital, we decided to stop on the way to look at a new tractor! It was an act of sheer defiance and therapy. For a time we were caught up with the world of grand machinery, sparkling new in green and gold.

Trembling, we went into the hospital the following week for the huge operation. Afterwards he was in Intensive Care for a day and a half before we received the specialist's diagnosis back in a hospital room. We both thought it was the beginning of the end. We were trying to be brave but this was epic.

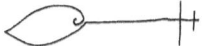

The task feels enormous. The moment does not always come with clarity for everyone, but at some stage the dreaded question must be faced: Will they live or die?

Waiting in Limbo

Waiting for an answer can seem endless. You seem to spend your days waiting. Waiting for the next thing. Waiting for test results, waiting for doctors or specialist appointments and visits, waiting for the next phone call, for some clarity ... anything to give a shred of hope. It can be like torture some days. At other times a few long awaited words from a doctor brings some relief. We take a next hopeful step. While it is hard on you, it can be harder for your loved-one, if they are conscious.

Concerned family members phone wanting news. I tell them the details that I know, all the small bits that have happened since we last spoke which doesn't satisfy them just as it left me wanting too. But it's all I have. Sometimes there is something more substantial and I share the information in full detail. Perhaps they'll pick up something I missed.

This limbo-waiting state can be brief or go on for a long time. Best to get used to it, get used to the not-knowing. Used to living with that unthinkable question: Is my loved-one really going to die? There is always something else the doctors can try—another procedure, a new drug, rest and a specific diet. Wait and see how this next step goes.

If they live, how long will they live for? How much longer will you have together? Six months? Two years? Or will this treatment be the cure so you can live out your full lives together? The worst part for me was I could see Martin going slowly downhill. I saw it in subtle ways day by day. His nights had been troubled over several years with sleeplessness and nightmares and he would wake me in the night for company. The family believed he was getting better because he rallied and put on a brave face when they visited, then collapse for days afterward to recover.

Other more practical concerns can plague you as well, although you wish they would just go away. Like how to cope with life without the beloved. You may have financial worries and your security may be in jeopardy. You may stand to lose your home, work, business, status, or your community by having to move. You might have your own health concerns or family problems to deal with. There may be a loss of purpose that came from your relationship as partner, parent, child, sibling or significant friend. If you are a parent, life without your child may be too much to contemplate.

Sleepless

Again you wake up
in the morning blackness
to echoes in your dream
and things that make you cry.
Next night you wake up
the inner fire no dream
but a dreaded living force.
Again it makes you cry.

Wondering whether they will die may be what we dare not say out loud, just in case we jinx it—superstitious or not, why risk it? Just in case the family is not up to hearing it said, or they feel unable to talk about it, to consider it. It can be a lonely place for our loved-one, whether they are an adult or child, if they don't have an opening to talk about this question. It may be up to you to introduce it in a gentle way and help them say what they want when they are ready.

Harbouring that question on your own is a lonely road to walk. Sometimes there are not too many other options. To put the question directly to the doctors rarely gets a direct, unambiguous answer. Maybe the medical experts just don't know. It could be they know enough not to say when it's the worst news, because miracles in the form of an extended lifetime do happen. Or they don't want to preempt your upset. Most doctors are more likely to talk about the next available step possible in treatment than to answer that question, even when the next step is just keeping them alive with deceasing quality of life. In reality, no one knows or can give an answer about when it will happen until the final stages of life are reached.

Children can sometimes be overlooked at this time. As adults, and especially as parents, we want to protect children from grief and pain, but in our concern we can isolate them by not giving them a way to talk about dying and express their feelings. Dying children can be closer to their soul than adults and surprisingly sensitive to the situation and its existential aspects, knowing precisely what is going on without being told explicitly. That was my and others experience as a child, which I expand on later in Chapter 6, Never Too Late to Say Goodbye. When that is the case, trying to protect a child from the truth may only serve to isolate them.

The possibility of losing your beloved may go in and out of awareness or be constantly in your mind. As our loved-one changes before our eyes, we are being changed as well as we witness it.

Here I am in intensive care. My mind about to explode. It's been two agonisingly long nights now. I watch her little body lying so still, so passive. Doctors and nurses check the machines and charts and do their work. Vigilant. Impressive. We are in their hands.

It's touch and go. As I sit quietly on my chair out of the way, I pray to God their healing magic is working.

A hole in the heart. I never knew. How could I have known? Is it my fault that has brought her to this? Jen, my wife, has gone for a break, down to the hospital coffee shop. She deserves it, this has been hard on her. If I was a woman I'd be able to cry. But I feel stunned inside. Gutted. That's my baby girl there on the ICU bed. My heart is breaking.

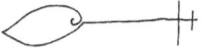

My wife has been sick for fifteen months. Finally knowing my sweet wife is to die, that she is dying now, is a relief. I feel bad saying that. I think only someone in my position would understand. It has been the uncertainty that got to me. What if I had to brace myself for a prolonged, drawn-out time while she suffered on and on, way off into the future? If she wasn't to die, that's what it would mean. But what would that really mean? It would be a very drawn-out, bad time ahead for both of us.

I am tired. Bone tired. The very thought of this situation going on for a prolonged time, with the reality of the care she needs and thinking I don't know how I can give her that care any more. Even with hired help. Just thinking about it makes me feel swamped, like I'll break down. That's a big admission for a man like me who has hardly cried since he was a little kid.

Thinking about the future if she were to live on is like the last ounces of my own life would be wrung out of me. And I feel so bad for thinking that way, because I still really love this woman. She is the love of my life. Probably now more than ever before. I don't want the agony of her suffering any more. It's enough.

Burn Out and the Need for a Break

Not knowing what will happen takes its toll. It becomes draining, especially as this can stretch out over many days, weeks or even months and longer. Medication can extend life in terminal illnesses for years. As we all try our best to stay balanced, loving and alert to new information as it comes to light, energy levels slowly deplete.

We soldier on. We do what needs to be done. We show up. Often, we don't sleep well, don't eat well and don't rest our minds from the turmoil of it all. Be aware of the symptoms of burnout and take responsibility for yourself (look more closely at Burnout and Overwhelm in Part IV). This is not the time to think or act as though you are invincible.

Short breaks every day help. Do something that clears the mind or distracts, just for a while. Walk through a busy market, a street or park; dance wildly at home; have a massage; take the dog for a walk; watch a sitcom. Take a break from the responsibility of your loved-one being at home, or from the noise and routine of hospital and clinical care. We pay a cost for being there with no time out to replenish: a deterioration in wellbeing, health, personal balance or life-force. Jen, the mother of a young child, was exhausted by worry, lack of sleep, and a compelling need to stay in Intensive Care after her little girl's operation.

At first, she had great hope after her little girl's heart operation. The doctors had been crystal clear about the outcomes and there were three possibilities: the child would make a full recovery; she would be dependent on a machine to keep her alive; or she would not survive the operation. Well, she was through the operation! Now it was a matter of waiting to see if it would be the worst or the best option.

Time dragged on and Jen stayed by her unconscious daughter's side in Intensive Care. Everywhere Jen looked was a constant confrontation with desperate life and death struggles. The smells, sounds and conversations were all clinical, measured, precise. Some nurses were so kind. Even so, ICU made Jen anxious and she became unable to make basic decisions, like whether to shift the car to avoid getting a parking ticket.

Jen and her husband left the hospital for home at about 9.30 each night, to return at 7am. On the morning of day three in ICU Jen became stressed with fears for her daughter's life. She realised the place itself escalated her anxiety levels through the roof. As soon as her husband came in Jen went out for a break, down to the cafe for well over an hour. There she had a long phone call with a close friend which settled her down. Jen's friend got to her see she was not helping the situation by adding her own stress. She needed to keep a clear mind as there might be a huge decision ahead about life support. The friend advised (actually told) Jen to take a cafe break and call a friend every few hours, and more often if she felt scared or overwhelmed.

That is sound advice for us all. Fears tend to rear up during the waiting time, whether you are together or partly separated from your loved-one because they are in hospital or rehabilitation. Realise that if you let fears go unchecked they start to take over. That is why it is important to step back to see what is happening and create some distance. There is a distinction between a problem and a big emotion, and whatever you do, don't feed and foster fears. In fact, do the opposite and go out of your way to stay calm and steady.

After eight gruelling days of touch and go, their little girl turned the corner and was on the way to recovery. They are the lucky ones.

Receiving Sudden News

Not everyone has the time or opportunity to say goodbye. Fatal accidents and suicide come out of the blue. Sudden death is traumatic for those left behind to receive the news, igniting immediate physical and emotional responses. The shock hits like a ten-ton truck, throwing us straight into a no-man's-land. The first reaction is trying to understand the message and then total disbelief that death has occurred, and often a conviction that it must be a mistake or not real. How could it be possible? Initially, the news is incomprehensible. Then confusing or numbing.

According to Kate Braestrup, a chaplain in Maine, USA, an authority working with sudden death bereavement, the physical responses to the news vary from yelling and wailing, to being frozen to the spot. Then an inability to talk, sleep, eat, heart palpitations, nervousness and exhaustion. Once the initial shock passes, many people settle themselves for an initial period. Braestrup found that once the immensity of what has happened is faced, then people become quieter. The rational mind takes over as an initial coping response, but as in Post Traumatic Stress Syndrome, the psychological response can rebound later if undermined in its significance.

It is hard and painful to accept that a loved-one's life has suddenly ended or is drawing to a close. The next life phase for us begins some time after our loved-one's departure. What it will be is yet to unfold, hard to bear thinking about and may seem overwhelming to face. The day to day stress and demands of your situation can be underestimated especially if you don't have someone to lean on and talk to, so stressful thoughts tend to turn inward on yourself. Experiencing survival and safety fears at this time is not unusual — after all, your world is being suddenly changed in many ways. Everyone needs some support and there are no medals for doing it all alone.

Clearing and Nurturing

You and your loved-one may already have had open conversations about death and dying, particularly when it's a life-long relationship or there has been a long illness. You may have covered subjects and questions like: What would one of you do if the other were to die?

There are things significant for you that you may want to talk about with them now, when the time seems right. There are practicalities, such as what your loved-one wants for burial, the estate and financial practicalities. In addition, the exchange of feelings is so important, in particular gratitude, appreciation, acknowledgement and recalling happy times together. You could say how much you will miss them, reassure them that they will remain in your heart, and you will manage through the grief process.

Grief is difficult to experience, especially for those who were told or shown as children that showing sadness is showing weakness. We can be unaware of sadness buried inside, but if we are human, it will be there from loss. Grief is a process that often starts with denial, or looking outside the self with mixed feelings like helplessness, confusion or blame. Grief takes many forms beside sorrow, from guilt to shame or anxiety. These feelings don't last forever, they rise up and fade away again. Experiencing unusually strong emotions is an indication the grieving process has started. At its most intense, it may seem like being thrown around in a washing machine or like living under a cloud of dread. Whatever you are experiencing, keep in mind grief needs attention. Grief needs you to nurture it with kindness.

Being together now is a time to listen wholeheartedly to your loved-one and say what is in your heart. When you are alone is a time for soulwork and nurturing yourself. The keys of soulwork, the work of the inner pilgrimage, are described in Part II, Second threshold Pilgrimage, while healing with nurturing rituals and practices are outlined in Part IV. Now we turn to being the dying companion.

Chapter 2

Becoming a Dying Companion

During the dying journey, moments of shared love have us feeling that our heart may burst. There comes a moment of knowing. Time together is running out. Either there is confirmation from an external source or an undeniable feeling from within that our loved-one is, in fact, now dying. At that point you may become their dying companion.

> I had been agonising over whether he was dying for many months. I was desperate for clarity. He would go downhill, then seemed to turn a corner and be on the mend again for a while before another downturn. Emotionally it had been a two-year-long roller-coaster ride. I was fatigued and weary of the emotional turmoil. I had become worn out by the illness dominating our lives. Then I felt ashamed, guilty. I didn't tell anyone about that.
>
> The moment of realisation came to my husband one morning: he was dying. It is such a clear picture in my memory. It was the moment he saw this illness was different. This time there would be no recovery. There was no way out.

Death was imminent. His voice was forced, his face set—

"How can anyone come back from something like this?!"

We both just looked at each other. The truth of those words rang out. He had waited to say them until I was near the end of his hospital bed, on my way to the bathroom. Somehow the distance was important. Like someone digging for complements, I felt he was digging for reassurance. Pleading. It was as though he was making a last stand, daring something or someone—me—to come along and save him. But I couldn't save him. It filled me with overwhelming grief.

Surrender was not yet there for him and he went in and out of an internal battle to hang on to life. But I surrendered at that time and accepted that he was dying. My acceptance was total and instinctual. The doctors and specialists would not say so, not until the very last. Yet to know, to hear it from them sooner would have given me the relief that comes with surrender. Grief surfaced from the depths where it had been lurking for months, haunting my life.

I resolved to take one small step at a time, just the next little step as it came up, whatever it was. Mainly, I resolved to be there for him. Just be there. And with that, some courage stirred and started to rise. This time, Martin had been in hospital nearly a month. I resolved to be with him full-time and not leave him alone at night ever again. Whatever it took, I would make it happen. Wherever he wanted to be, here in the hospital or in a hospice. Whatever was possible. I just followed my gut.

Through trial and error I found that previous patterns of our relationship no longer applied and the way we talked together now was different. Being the hero wasn't important anymore for Martin and he was more relaxed and open about his vulnerability. That made it easier for me to know what he wanted.

Moving into his hospital room full-time turned out to be the best, most loving thing I could have done. It was his silent plea.

A Dying Companion, the Torch Holder

It can be easy to feel uncertain about becoming a dying companion when we don't know what to do or what to expect at the moment of death, if we are present. I felt that way as my life partner was relying on me and so much seemed to be at stake.

As the dying journey progressed, I slowly became his dying companion. It was a shift from being his intensive carer for a year and a half to a different relationship, especially over all the time he was in hospital. The realisation he might die had occurred to me months beforehand; now there was an acceptance and surrender it was inevitable. The energy between us changed. The energy lay with me. He became the passive beloved, while I was the active giver of love and hope, as though I held up a little light. Our relationship became elevated, practicalities faded and we related spiritually.

As the dying companion we become the Torch Holder. This is of the greatest significance to the one dying, even though it may never be made explicit. The energy changes and being close is paramount, if not literally close for various reasons (such as it may not be possible to be with them through the day), then symbolically and virtually close. They want you with them now. Being with the dying passage can't help but involve intense awareness and sensitivity from the depths of the soul. We may not be always physically present but are in their heart and mind and walk the path with them emotionally. Whatever our relationship has been, the one dying is drawn to us now. They choose us.

This shift from the normal, everyday to the spiritual is not uncommon for the one dying, nor for the dying companion and seems to come naturally like an old friend. Any apprehension about the dying process can be soothed through the depth experienced between the two of you. It is a beautiful gift for your loved-one and to yourself. A long time ago when people died at home, the whole family gathered around and provided comfort and support to the one dying and each other. Past generations handed down all the ritual and pathway for dying to the family and community, so there were known ways to proceed. Today, with so few people dying at home, being a dying companion doesn't have any pathway or set of rituals to follow, but we can recreate them together.

Beautiful Endings

We can make the dying time a beautiful ending. A beautiful ending isn't all lovely with choirs singing and harps playing. There is still the pain and grief of loss. A beautiful ending is a state of mind, a light to keep us sane and safe and centred as we go through the dying passage with our loved-one—and beyond, to help our grieving process and recovery. A beautiful ending means facing the loss of a loved-one and life without them, by seeking a sense of beauty as part of the dying time.

Being able to see and experience beauty is healing and gently transcendent. Beauty takes us to the realm of the sacred and wonder, and forms a warm blanket of protection around us. It is a sanctuary. This has been what I discovered during the dying and loss of people I love, and I have seen beauty work in this way for others. A beautiful ending is healing. While standing in the fire is the emotional experience of grief, a beautiful ending is the possible outcome. Beauty and love reside with heartbreak.

A beautiful ending can be learned and embraced, it is something we make and rarely one that simply happens due to good circumstances or a turn for the better. The dying passage can be anxious, disorienting, challenging and sometimes traumatising. These feelings are tamed by a shift away from the anxious thoughts and imaginings linked to the feelings to concentrate instead on what is beautiful—how much you mean to each other, that you need each other for this dying time, your souls are connected, and dying is natural and a time of grace, sometimes with much feeling. There is healing in this. Trauma can be overtaken and soothed by healing.

Making a beautiful ending relies on three things:

The intention to make it a beautiful ending. During the dying passage, whether it is days or months, you become the torchholder for making a beautiful ending. That means there must first be acknowledgement that your loved-one is now in their dying time. We must face the truth. When it was my husband's time, his doctor told us both together although we each knew innately for weeks beforehand. If only you have been given this information and your loved-one asks, be honest. Face it directly. There is no need to pretend there is yet another treatment to try or there could be a spontaneous recovery, because that shuts down speaking from the soul for both of you. And speaking from the soul is beautiful.

A commitment to be present psychologically, emotionally, soulfully. The notion of commitment cannot be underestimated. Once there is an open acknowledgement that their dying time has begun, let your loved-one know that, "We will go through this together". Internally, it is the commitment to be present with your loved-one. To say these simple words often, "We'll go through this together", eases you into being present, available and open. It frees you to be able to say when there are things you don't know, cannot know, but you don't know them together. It is a commitment to be there to share in their dying passage. This deepens trust and intimacy. It is the kind of healing that comes from the heart and soul.

A willingness to speak from your truth. To do this you must know your truth. Always, it comes from the heart. Your truth is different to blurting out how you feel or have felt in the past, particularly about a hurt or misunderstanding between you. Speaking your truth is considered and compassionate toward the one you are speaking to. What you say is not about you only but held in the context and deep bond of your relationship. The philosopher, Martin Buber, named this conversation "I-Thou" to distinguish it from an exchange of "I to You" when we tend to objectify the other and focus on getting our message across and not on more tender connecting threads between us. I-Thou is thoughtful and kind.

Flying

This is not the time
for recrimination
for regret of what was broken

It is their dying time

It is not the time
for asking why
for allocating blame
for not forgiving
for pushing back
for saying you're afraid
for conforming to anything

It is not the time
to show your broken wing

It is the time of giving
for the sake of their dying
and knowing
your own ways of flying
despite it all.

A Spiritual Relationship

The dying companion has a special relationship with the one dying. Religious or not, and whether loving, robust, full of fight, or eggshell walking, the dying time is spiritual. The commitment to be with them over the time of their dying passage may be implicit rather than spelt out between you. Your loved-one may ask you to spend more time with them, possibly express it as a wish. They may ask you to always be there for them or they rely on seeing you every day if they are in care or hospital. A dying companion can be full-time or part-time, and that can change along the way. If you can't be there in person, being there virtually online is an option.

How do you see being a dying companion? For me it was to be with my loved-one as much as possible (my husband wanted me there all the time, others wanted time alone), to be sensitive and receptive to their needs and feelings. Also, to check what conditions they wanted around them which could vary from day to day. I aimed to be there emotionally and spiritually to offer support, comfort and be their friend, to watch over them, to hear what they wanted to say, to sit silently with them, to be a soul witness to their last journey. It was a great privilege to be there during the dying time.

Martin said to me, "You are my anchor." It seemed strange that he would want stability and solidity after his life of impetuousness. It felt like walking with him on his dying path, a sacred witness bringing forth all of the soul I could muster.

I was not afraid. I didn't fear for Martin in his death, and with him I faced my own death in a way never before, slowly and without illusions. I wanted to be with him in this spiritual and total transformation. In the last few weeks he shifted in his attitude, as though from his ego to his soul. My mother did the same in her last days. I was glad to be there as he went through the stages of the dying passage, it was where I was meant to be and felt natural. However, Martin continued to fight as moments of panic beset him, "I'm slipping into a black hole. I can't get out." I wouldn't leave him, not knowing what to say. Then some words came, "I'm here with you. We're here together. It's all right", and I held him.

Unfortunately, there is fear and apprehension associated with dying. Death is not bad. It is inevitable and natural. Like birth, it creates the boundary that defines our life. Dying humans often have transcendent experiences of seeing truth and life clearly, sometimes with regret, sometimes with wisdom or gratitude for what has been. The privilege being with someone dying opens heart and mind to what is most real and valued in life. It cuts through the noise and peripheral stuff of daily life and takes us right to our soul, where there is no trauma. There are waves of deep feeling and insight that become a profound spiritual experience. It felt like time had paused.

The dying time before the end of life is often overlooked as a time of grieving, supposing that grief comes after the loved-one has gone. Yet the dying passage may be just as intense as bereavement following death. Through the dying time, there can be many eruptions of grief without any discrimination about where and when they take hold and are expressed. Through all the grief experienced, it was a time of increased affinity, truth-talking and compassion. I was at one with my soul.

Bearing Witness

Bearing witness to someone in their dying time is a moving experience. The notion of "bearing witness" seems to capture it, a responsibility of trust and one carried out in grace as we let the one dying take the lead.

To bear witness is to bear witness to yourself as well as your loved-one. It is like being the Zen observer—being detached while staying compassionate. Detachment does not mean becoming cut off, but we don't take on their suffering or become harrowed. The desire to console or try to rescue may be strong, yet it may not be what your loved-one wants or needs. It can be tricky to sort out your desire to care and protect, from seeing and hearing what your loved-one needs and is telling you. Intuition plays a part, as does asking: "I want to comfort you. Is that what you want, or do you need me to listen, just be here beside you?" Once aware of your own need and desire, you become free to ask and find the words to ask.

Bearing witness means being in the present, without judgement or a plan. It means getting out of the way with our own preconceptions, wishes and hopes. It means relinquishing control, and supporting our dying loved-one to be in the lead and know what is best for them. That can be a fine line to walk because sometimes they just don't know what is best and are gripped by precariousness. At those times we need compassion. We can take the loved-one by the hand and reassure, be their cloak of loving care and tell them it is all right. They are doing well. You are there for them, going through this with them. Compassion is needed for deep-seated fear if it rears up.

At other times when our loved-one is doing okay, we can gently follow them. It is their death and to do in their own way. That means giving up our ideas of what a "good death" is and of "dying well". Best selling author, Elizabeth Gilbert, talks of her beloved partner raging with torrid anger as she moved closer and closer to her death. It was excruciating for the dying companions, but an authentic expression of the lion-like person she was, while Gilbert bore deep witness.

Healthcare Professionals as Dying Companions

Healthcare professionals sometimes become dying companions. Where would we be without them? This is especially so when family cannot attend the patient, or when the patient has no close family. Whist palliative carers are specifically trained to care for the needs of the dying, nurses as the daily carers are not. At least, not in the same way. According to a study by Hermann, and another by Drury and Hunter, many nurses are left uncertain and uncomfortable with the emotional and spiritual needs of their dying patient. Spiritual needs are identified in the study as distinct from religious needs, and include needing to complete unfinished business, experience nature, and a need for positive outlook.

Health professionals face some added complications of potential role conflict and confusion with other healthcare disciplines, where responsibilities can be blurred. The amount of time they are able to spend with a patient depends on competing needs of other patients and being able to juggle the other demands of their job.

A great deal is asked of our healthcare professionals. They do their best under demanding conditions to give holistic, patient-centred care, defined in the literature as "bio-psycho-socio-spiritual care". That is an enormous ask. I wonder how anyone can be expected to deliver and fulfil all that every day. Burnout would become prevalent, possibly an underground issue resulting in a loss of capability. Healthcare professionals must decide what aspects of care they are able to give within the boundaries and practicalities of their role, their own propensities and learning. A characteristic of burnout is constantly thinking they have not done enough for their patient and then overcompensating, driven by guilt to intensify their efforts. It is such a human thing to do, where compassion spills over into a lack of self-care.

Given all the demands of the work, I have seen heathcare professionals, especially nurses, take naturally to be openhearted dying companions. Somehow they find a way to fit it in, even if only for the short time periods they have available between other duties to stay with their patient.

Burnout causes some marvellous practitioners to leave their profession. It is a cycle of prolonged or intensive overwork and dedication to the job. Two things are common—not realising the risk that burnout is imminent, and not knowing how to break the cycle of overwork. Consequently, good people simply get used up.

Professional caregivers often walk a path that leaves no footprints behind except for the human rapport that occurs between patient and care-giver in the moment.

For some practical approaches and to keep self-care front of mind, see the Part IV sections on Burnout and Self-Care.

Your Loved-One's Needs

What would you want and need if it were you dying?

We all want a good death, to be peaceful, cocooned by love, care and appreciation, and to know our life had meaning. What meaning would you want for your life? Would you want to be regarded as a human of integrity, purpose and principle? Or know you had endearing ways such as a sense of humour and made others laugh and be happy? Perhaps you want to have achieved or contributed something significant or be remembered for your life's work? Or that you were loving, always including others to make them feel relaxed and welcome? Or you were a healer, or a teacher?

We are loved and remembered for our essence and it is our true gift. If we convey our gratitude for our loved-one's gift, their true essence, we will have done much to reassure them their life was worthwhile and has a lasting legacy, and they are special, important, and truly loved.

In considering our loved-one's needs when they are dying, we want to do whatever we can to help them die in a calm and peaceful state of mind. We can reassure them through our attitude, what we say and how we say it.   Let's have a brief look at some research and experiences of those who are dying.   Hermann's research into the needs of the dying concluded that dying humans have special needs, for the most part spiritual needs: "Spiritual needs of the dying were broad in scope and linked closely to purpose and meaning in life.".

One of the best things we can do is consider all the ways our loved-one's life has had meaning. Remind them of the positive things they have done in life or ask them to recount these things to you. As well as any accomplishments, affirm and talk about their distinctive qualities, such as magnanimity, kindness, generosity, compassion, creativity, gratitude, humility, resilience. Think about people they crossed paths with in projects, community, or as neighbours, and the way they assisted or lit up others' lives. Go over these memories together with your loved-one. Encourage them to remember stories and incidents or places. When possible, bring in photos (my stepson did this so beautifully) and bring messages from friends and past buddies. All this helps your loved-one remember what they did and meant to others, who they were and what they contributed at different phases of their life. This is important for children who are dying as well as adults, so they not only know they are well loved but also that their life has meaning.

Be open and receptive to what they want to say, which may include regrets and unfinished business. It is important not to protect them by using justifications or excuses which in effect pushes away their words and shuts down what else they want to say. Be with them openly, with an open and deep sharing of the person's memory, fear, pain, love, annoyance or whatever. It is unnecessary to talk much. Just listen. Later on, remind them of those who love them, warts and all.

For a religious person, some religious symbols in the room and inviting a member of their religious order to attend them could be beneficial, but ask them first to be sure.

Avoid people or activities that your loved-one does not want or are not appropriate. This could go against social or religious norms, but the dying process belongs to the one dying, not to those around them. Avoid people, ceremonies, music or items that your dying loved-one tells you, or you know, will provoke their anger, suffering or distress.

Clinging is overly strong attachment by others who cling to the one dying, making it hard for the loved-one to let go and die peacefully. As a dying companion we do not want to disturb the state of the dying person and so we do all we can to help them be in a calm, peaceful state of mind. While remaining receptive to our loved-one, we stay on the look out for what and who disturbs and upsets them.

Remind others ahead of time to be calm, explaining dying is the time to let go attachments. Disturbing shows of emotion in front of the loved-one opens up new business and attachment for the one dying to attend to. Instead, remind others to affirm and release the one dying. The dying process is of great spiritual significance and everyone can help the one dying to be increasingly clear and serene.

The dying person cannot take care of others and are no longer in a state to look after others' emotional needs. Visitors who spill out needy emotions (including irritation, clinging, sobbing and fear) must go elsewhere for their own needs and resolution. As dying companions, we may be the ones to get needy visitors out of the room, not to return or to emphasise why they cannot do that again.

Encourage others to do whatever they can to allow the dying person to die in a peaceful state of mind. For some, it means putting their own needs in second place and preparing themselves to be calm and receptive when they visit.

Being with them in silence. Amongst the spiritual teachings on death and dying, there is much mention of the mind becoming more subtle and receptive during the dying journey, see for example Sogyal Rinpoche's The Tibetan Book of Living and Dying. Dying humans are more open to receiving subtle messages from those close to them. That means as a dying companion, silent communication can be beneficial. Another way to look at it is you don't have to talk, just being there with them silently is enough. Touch becomes heightened.

Your blessing: remember you can give your blessing to your beloved. You can tell them they can let go, you will be all right. It can be a big release for them to feel secure that you love and cherish them and will go on without them, especially to carry on any legacy, offerings or ways of being you shared.

The Atmosphere for Dying

From time to time it is a relief to have a beneficial task to perform. Just some simple things make all the difference. Keep in mind the most precious thing you have to offer is your self, not filling the space with activities and distractions. The spaciousness and value of time is everything. These are some additional ideas and gifts to offer for the days that seem long.

Music
Bring in well-loved music. Before you play it, ask if they want to hear that particular music now, because their preferences while dying can change. If they are not conscious, play only soothing music and play it very softly.

Candles
Candles give a softer, gentler light that is a rest from hasher artificial light. Candlelight is conducive to the inner world which includes the gentle world of spirituality. Candles are symbolic and the spirit is often described as a flame.

Readings
Read from a novel, a short story or some poetry. Read slowly. Choose material that is positive and reassuring, speaking of truth.

Friends

If it is the loved-one's wish, invite friends to come and say goodbye. Fill them in on how long to stay and give them a hint on what they might say, for instance, it would be good if you reminisce on happy times or what you learned, how you were helped and your gratitude.

Massage

Massage can be soothing, just be clear they are up to it and it is what they want, not only what you want to give. Find out what sort of massage they want—a foot massage, hands, head. Also find out whether they want you giving the massage or a masseur used to palliative care.

Loving Images

Bring loving images and photos from their life into the room. My step son assembled photos of the family and the farm playing on a tablet. More abstract images are soothing, such as beautiful scenes from nature, skyscapes or oceans.

Guided Meditation

There are some lovely meditations available online for relaxation and long ones for sleep, some run for hours and are calming and restful. Try looking up "sleep meditations". Be clear this is what your loved-one wants. If you are practiced at working with guided meditations or guided fantasy and want to do your own, a peaceful meditation is to imagine a glow of loving light surrounding the one dying.

Stories

Ask them to tell stories from their life or tell stories yourself of events, situations or people that they have carried in their heart. Ask for their life story. Ask if you can record it or note it down.

Hands

Never underestimate the calming power of simply holding the hand of your loved-one. Even if your family and relationship has not been demonstrative, there are often new needs for touch that arise for the dying, so try out a brief touch first, watch for their response. Lightly stroking their arm or hair, a kiss on the forehead or hand may be enough.

Learning As We Go Along

Looking back on the dying time and re-reading my journal, I recall my dread for what was coming, my alert watchfulness, and longing. It was an extreme and persistent journey with bittersweet experiences that left me feeling emptied out. During the last few months I lost my appetite, leaving me physically emptied out, eating only tiny amounts each day. The physical emptying matched my inner sense of emptying out. It was a symptom of grief. Given the magnitude of the change occurring, some inner echo and reaction was no surprise.

In amongst my journal notes I see attempts to give myself advice to keep a grip and try to make sense of being swept along by a massive current. This advice was a way of being more positive than berating myself. It would come up during morning reflections or contemplating an incident I could have handled better. I wrote in the third person, talking to myself. (Sometimes, I just needed to get over myself.)

Instructions to Myself

Listen well to the things your loved-one says. Listen for the subtext and feeling tone.

Take the lead. Spell out what seems to be being asked for, or what your intuition indicates. When a regular visitor depresses the loved-one, say, "What would it be like if I asked that person not to visit anymore?"

Check your decisions and actions will be welcomed by your loved-one, don't assume. Even though you know them well, allow for their preferences to change during the dying time.

When you can't check, follow instinct and intuition.

Taking action motivates courage. The right action will be welcomed by your loved-one. It can be trial and error. It's all right.

Be **kind to yourself.** There will be times you feel you let your loved-one down, or let yourself down. Be gentle with yourself.

More than anything else, **just be there.** Just listen. Keep your heart open.

I came to realise, and this may not be for everyone, that devotion was the final stage of love. Devotion is what is needed as the dying companion, and within that is love and soul.

Occasionally I was surprised that amidst grief, I was still able to feel a fleeting moment of happiness that popped up out of the blue. This is from my journal during the dying process.

> In the midst of my grief while my husband is dying, I watch two tiny birds land on the edge of the little birdbath that is left in the shade of a golden-leafed tree. One bird stood guard. The other hopped in, light as a feather, splashing and dancing in the water, wings spread wide to show iridescent colours. They are beautiful, and with surprise, I realise I am happy.

Toxic Behaviour

If the one dying is loving and sweet, it may be overwhelmingly heart-wrenching for you at this time. However, if they are filled with rage, disappointment and bitterness, verbally lashing out at others and at you in particular, as in the following story, then you need some protection and a chance to replenish yourself.

It was Craig's third day in hospital after his heart attack. The prognosis was bleak. Retirement was to be his best time of life; he was entitled to it and didn't hold back his anger and foul mouth at this attack spoiling it. His wife, May, shrank back under the onslaught of his ranting. She was silenced by him within a few minutes of arrival in his hospital room. He called the doctors incompetent fools and blamed nurses for his deteriorating health. May followed them out of the room to apologise and found one of the nurses sobbing. She was the same age their own daughter would have been if she had not died as a baby. As May consoled her she realised all the things she said to the nurse applied equally to herself. "Refuse to take his bad temper. Stand up to him. He is the one dependent on you. Don't let him get to you—just ignore his ugly words."

May went for a walk. Outside the apple blossom was falling. She listened to the bees and stood in the breeze and remembered being a teenager, wilful and free. Walking back into Craig's hospital room later, May stood straight. "I will sit with you for a while today, Craig. The minute you start with your foul language and abuse, I'm out that door. Then I may or may not come back tomorrow."

Toxic behaviour from a loved-one affects us differently. We can put up with it and not take it to heart. We empathise and understand their anguish and overwhelm as they realise they are at the end of the road and their life is nearly over. Their regrets and burning resentments are unleashed. That only goes so far, and when the behaviour is more than an outburst and it persists, leaving you hurt and distressed, you need to protect yourself.

Clearing the mind, then setting a boundary about what you will no longer put up with and holding firm is a way to go, but some preparation may be needed. Some ways to stay on your side of the fence and set limits can be found in Rituals and Contemplations, see A Shielding Meditation.

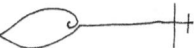

Becoming a dying companion may not appeal to you or may be the last thing you feel able to do. If you have misgivings about going through the dying time with your loved-one, consider whether you are underestimating your capacity and inner resources. There are no right or wrong ways to be with someone who is dying, no matter how close you are in kinship or friendship. Sometimes it is something that just does not seem the right path.

Simone was in her sixties and for decades had looked after her ageing mother, who was needy and demanding. They didn't live together, but Simone felt abused and manipulated by her mother who had a long history of mental illness. After her mother had a stroke, Simone went to the hospice daily to see her dying mother for twenty minutes, sometimes an hour. She would sit by the bed and hold her mother's hand. There wasn't much to say and her mother was rarely awake. The hospice staff gently encouraged Simone to stay longer. "There's a coffee machine and a cafe for family. It's really very comfortable and peaceful." Still, Simone was very clear she would not—could not—spend more time with her mother. Simone made sure she was comfortable and well looked after, but felt unable to give anything more. Her reserves were depleted.

All of us do what we do at the time, in relationship with the one who is dying. Don't beat yourself up if in hindsight you wish you could have handled it differently. It may well be that what you did or did not do was just right, just what your loved-one needed, and balanced what you needed. There are no rules. No one really knows. I asked my husband about most things, but not all, because he wasn't really up to making many decisions or choices anymore. Even simple things like, "Do you want your music on now?" Sometimes he would say, "You decide," or "I don't care." So, I aimed to be sensitive, put my trust in our relationship and how well we knew each other, and hoped that would support the situation. I trusted myself to pick up his reactions as we went along to guide me. Everything was flexible. Anything decided could be reversed, changed.

Grieving Together

A most beautiful, spontaneous thing can be grieving together. You and your loved-one. It is a time of abundant kindness and sharing. Truths may need to be shared and memories of happy times. Say whatever words of love and loss are needed. This is a sacred time, and grieving with each other is a sacred part of your goodbyes. It is truly making beautiful music together.

The dying time is precious time together. You can use that time in a way that supports you both. Reading the following poem is a way of recalling and talking about memories and loving times shared together.

Let's

Let's remember laughing so freely
there's no censorship
just free together
Let's recall walking all that time ago
with friends and in places
Let's bring those silken threads to us now
and weave them into this moment

Let's become self-luminous,
can you imagine that . . . ?
so that love and ecstasy
outshine the loveless self
to relax the knot at our centre
and allow all this to unfold.

Befriended by ways of life
and taught by ways of death
Let's be self-liberating
flooded by what is radiant
not brutal and sad
but what is raw and wondrous

Let's make the choice
the high road or low road
Let's accept the truth
of this most prescious time.
Let's become flooded with love
and refuse fear.

Chapter 3

Gone: The Loss of Your Loved One

The time arrives for your loved-one to die, although we don't know that ahead of time. Not everyone can be there at the time of death, nor wants to be. Sometimes the dying person has not been conscious for some time, but awake most want the reassurance and courage of having you with them holding hands. Anticipating being present for their death might feel epic beforehand. What can you expect? Will the time of death be traumatic? Or painful for your loved-one. Will you be able to bear it? Will it claim and colonise the rest of your life? Here are some experiences that others have shared.

> What should I expect? I didn't know but I was there when she died. I wanted to be there although I was really worried about it, mega nervous, in fact. It was something I had never done before and I knew nothing about it. But her passing away was very peaceful. There was no hardship or bother. Her eyes were closed all morning and her breathing was very slow with a long time in between breaths. Then, there wasn't another breath. She had just drifted off. I felt peaceful too

and so glad I was there with her. It was very serene.

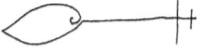

It was a relief. I feel guilty for feeling relieved. But it's true. I do. I don't let anyone know that's what I think. Oh, God, it has been so hard. Such a huge thing. When I realised she had a stroke, my heart started to sink. It was the one thing she was always most afraid of. Ever since we first met all those years ago. Having a stroke and being left a vegetable. Unable to look after herself. For someone who was so independent, that would have been sheer hell. For both of us.

Don't get me wrong, I miss her with every bone of my body. I'm devastated. But filled with gratitude at the same time. I have no idea how I'll cope. How I'll pick up the pieces. What gives me strength is at the last, just before she died, she seemed to regain her senses. For the first time since the stroke she looked straight at me and said, "I'll watch over you." I will forever be blown away by the hugeness of that and her loving thought of me in her last moment.

One autumn morning, as the world awoke from its darkness and filled again with birdsong and colour, my love opened his eyes and took his last slow breath.

For weeks I had been with him while normal life was long ago suspended. Being there soothed his fears and the demons not faced in life. He said, "You're my rock. You keep me from falling into a black void." This sort of talk was not like him. Neither was asking his doctor four weeks ago for medication to lift his mood. "I'm getting depressed, doc."

We had a pact. Whichever one of us were to die first would

send a sign to the other. If we felt fulfilled we would die looking up, that was the sign that we were ascending, feeling love and peace. The realisation that Martin had just died, slowly became insistent as I studied him for signs of life. I looked for breath that was no more. The reality that he had died was not quite believable. Nevertheless, I looked to his eyes.

Where had he been looking? Could it be slightly upwards or was it straight ahead? I got up and looked at him from different angles, aware there was something Monty Python in my antics. Pretty well straight ahead. Did that mean he was trying to look up when his eyes relaxed to a resting position? Or was sending me a sign the furthest thing from his mind? Of course I will never know but I hope he ascended into death with a full heart.

It was 5am. I sat quietly with him for over an hour until Narelle, the nurse on morning shift, came in. "Good morning. How are we today?" Her voice was cranked up decibels louder than necessary and it crashed through the peace and quiet. "Could you speak more quietly please, Narelle?" But she did not pay much attention to me as she inspected the empty drip and its tubes. "This batch is empty. I'll replace it for you." Then Narelle looked at Martin, noticing he had not replied. "Martin . . . Martin . . . Can you hear me, Martin?!"

"Please. Just leave him be." Ignoring me, she checked for his pulse. Twice. Then tried to speak to him again in a voice that would normally wake the dead. "Martin?" Somehow it seemed like a transgression, disturbing the quiet. Finally she said, "I think he has gone. I'll get the ward sister."

"There's no need. Just leave him alone. His doctor needs to see him, to confirm." All I wanted was some uninterrupted peace. But there was more bustle and noise with the head nurse and Narelle coming back, checking there were no vital signs, fussing with the drip and other equipment. Finally the nurses left.

We don't really know at what point death occurs, and some research has found brain activity and a form of consciousness goes on for some time after vital signs stop. Many cultures and traditions follow this, and believe the person's soul or consciousness does not leave straight away. It was very important that I not leave him on his own. The hospital staff were kind and said there was no hurry, the room was not needed.

So while Martin stared out at nothing I continued to talk to him. Just in case his consciousness lingered. Just in case the message got though. I was struggling to accept the reality. I told him what an exceptional life he lived. That his work moved and helped many people, he is well-loved and assured him that would not change because he is no longer alive and with us. I blessed him. I blessed the time we had together in life. I blessed our home and family. I wept tears from my soul for the next eight hours. Grief and the stress of the last eight months poured out. During that time alone with him, I was able to say my last goodbye.

My lovely daughter came to pick me up. I was so happy to see her, to be cared for so lovingly. I felt depleted and disoriented. What had happened seemed profound. My life was totally changed, like turning a sudden corner into a completely different landscape. Those long hours with Martin were immensely sad, sacred and beautiful.

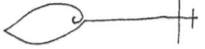

It is often said that some humans wait until they are alone to die. Such was the case in the next story when an old lady died the way she wanted and had always predicted, "with her boots on" and doing what she loved. It is a story told to me simply and with love. Perhaps because the two family members were not with her when she died, the symbols took on great importance and meaning for them.

My 97-year-old grandmother was strong as an ox. After her husband died, she ran the farm on her own for twenty years. We were staying with her one rainy weekend. In between showers, Gran took off on the tractor. She was picking up the bales of hay one at a time and moving them from the paddock where they had been cut, into the hayshed. Another shower came and went and we realised she'd been gone a long time. We took off from the house to find her.

There she was, flat out on the hayshed floor beside the tractor that was still idling. Ben and I are both doctors so we had no trouble in establishing that our Gran was dead. We called an ambulance. This was exactly the way she wanted to go—with her boots on. With tears flowing we laid her body out on the hay bales and waited for the ambulance to arrive.

Rain was pouring down. Gran had been so excited about the rain because the country had been in drought for years. The dams were nearly empty. It rained so hard a waterfall cascaded over the hay shed roof while we looked out from inside. Gran would have loved that. Finally the deluge subsided and the rain stopped. As the sky cleared the most fabulous rainbow I'd ever seen appeared. Then I knew Gran was all right.

The Time of Death

There may be apprehension about being at our loved-ones death with its many unknowns including whether the experience is one we could regret. What will happen at the moment of death? Will there just be the two of us present? Do you want to be there? Will there be a death rattle? The idea of that unnerving last breath filled me with foreboding and I wondered if it was painful. I have never heard a death rattle with any of the deaths I have been present. Mainly it was "slipping away".

It's comforting to investigate what various philosophies and religions say about the dying process, and if you are interested I encourage you to read some reliable sources. In his classic text, Tibetan Buddhist Sogyal Rinpoche details the dying process, affirming it is of great significance spiritually for everyone. He describes the process of dying in eight cycles, distilled here:

First cycle: the element is earth: a cycle of simultaneous dissolution as the body (Its earth) weakens.

Second cycle: the element is water: bodily fluids and feelings accompanying sense consciousness start to cease.

Third cycle: the element is fire: the mindfulness (fire) of affairs and people close fade, the sense of smell and digestion cease.

Fourth cycle: the element is wind: the body winds (body energies) move to the heart; breathing ceases. There is no awareness of external physical actions.

Fifth cycle to Eighth cycle: internal winds (energies) shift from the heart to other chakras, ending with a "life-bearing wind in the indestructible drop in the heart". At this point the dying person experiences the *mind of clear light* of death. There is no fear, but transcendence.

Buddhist ideology continues about the soul or pure consciousness which then awaits reincarnation, the time the soul enters another in utero for the continuing journey of consciousness development. Reincarnation continues for many lifetimes until enlightenment is reached. Once enlightenment is reached, the final physical death is undergone in the highest state of consciousness. Buddhists have a beautiful belief of the rainbow body for the death of great masters, men and women. The masters have reached an absence of delusion and an attainment of truth with practices of pure light. During death, the attainment of the rainbow body is accompanied by the physical appearance of light and rainbows.

The time at death and just afterward is peak intensity. We need time to sit with what has happened, just to take it in. Most of us know that nothing can last forever and everything will come to an end. We know it but may not believe it. We pledge to be with a life-partner until death yet say we will love each other forever. Even though endings are inevitable, when they come they affect us in ways both powerful and far reaching.

The Last Breath

His mind was clear
while his body died
and sleep overtook.
Then for two days
I hardly made a sound
not knowing
what to expect
still saying inside,
I'm not afraid.

His last breath gone
I held his hand
for hours and said,
It is all right
you are well loved,
lived a big life and
were so brave.
Take your time
leaving now.
I am here for you
until your soul
forever
flies away.

The Shock of Absence

The emptiness never leaves you. At first, you can't get away from it. In the shower. Driving the car. Watching the news. Cooking an egg. Tasting a ripe pear. Hearing the phone ring. There is no forgetting. No respite even for a moment. They are gone. This is true whether you must return to a home you shared together or you go elsewhere, perhaps you didn't live together.

It remains unbelievable. Logically you know what has happened and may be making the funeral arrangements. Yet there's another part of you that cannot quite comprehend it all. How can they simply be gone? It seems impossible; they have literally disappeared into thin air.

Their absence is everywhere. In the places that you used to meet, in your home. The chair they always sat in is forever empty. The voice that filled the room is missing. Their reading glasses lie abandoned on the table, just where they left them. Their shoes, coat, clothes, coffee mug, car—everything that was theirs sits there uninhabited and neglected. It is disturbing and strange, like being in a disconcerting dreamworld.

The Little Things

Little things between two people who know each other very well suddenly stop, and we can't get away from the reminders. There is no breathing space or intermission. While your loved-one was sick, these things diminished or were placed on hold, or they became staccato, reduced to certain hours of the day when visitors were allowed, or when your loved-one felt up to it. But once they die and are gone, all these small, everyday intimacies that were taken for granted are gone too. The ones only you shared together, life-partner, parent or child, all the banal things in life, like finding out how their day went; saying the computer is playing up again; or how you helped an old man across the road today; or you spilt coffee on your best shirt—suddenly they are not there anymore to share all the trivia of life. It's not the sort of thing to phone someone to tell them about. It's just what you share with someone close. It forms the fabric and music of life together. It is sharing. It is listening, showing care, laughing.

In the Celtic language of Ireland, according to poet Pádraig Ó Tuama, there are no words for being in love. Instead, they say something so beautiful:

"You are my music."

The music between people doesn't diminish just because they are gone. It strengthens. Like a cello and guitar playing together, one deepened what the other contributed. One started off and the other joined and replied. One person sleeps, the other watching over them sleeping. One person lies dying, the other watches over their safe journey. The music is the space in between, made of the love between the two. This in-between space is where you flourish in your inner beauty.

After such beautiful intimacy, gone forever seems unbelievable. There don't seem to be other words for it and the realisation keeps coming in waves, over and over.

Sometimes, Grief Can Be Harsh

Families have their own ways of dealing with loss and grief, but it can be very tough for some when there is an accumulation of pain left unresolved from the past. That makes it difficult or beyond them to comfort and support each other. The fear of the floodgates opening can be overwhelming and cause everyone to block sharing feelings or memories. I was left feeling heavy-hearted for the isolation and suffering of the family in this story.

> We don't talk about it in our family. Once the funeral was over and we sent a reply note to people who came, some who hardly knew her, others who really mourned her passing . . . once all that finished she wasn't mentioned again at home. Or anywhere, for that matter. It was as though a blanket of

silence was thrown over us all, as though we all looked the other way. All her things were cleared out quickly and gone. You wouldn't know she ever existed, except for my brother and me as her children. He's gone along with it, though, and shut the door on talking about her. Like dad.

I'd wake up at 1am. Then lie there with thoughts racing around. It is so painful. I loved mum so much. I can't bear her gone. My anguish goes on and on, maybe I'm half asleep, maybe not. I'd look at the clock. Nearly 2am. I force myself to go back to sleep. I toss and turn for hours. 3.30am. I wrap myself in the bedclothes and cry. At 5am I get up. It goes on like that night after night.

Quietly as I can, I wash and dress in the dark. Don't risk going to the kitchen for tea. Someone might hear. I can't let the others know. That would be shameful. They would find it disdainful that I'm upset and can't sleep. They might turn their back on me. Then where would I be? I force myself to think of the day, get my torch and write a list. Daylight comes. I start to feel better.

I go to the kitchen and make tea. Not a trace of her—and yet she is still everywhere. In every room there are reminders of her, especially here, in this room, as though she's just around the corner, about to walk in. I look at her chair and the physical pain of grief rushes back. The others come in. We go on walking around each other without eye contact. Just saying the necessities, some details about the day. As though she was never there.

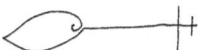

Grief is private. For families who were not good at talking about their emotions and have learned to be stoic, the result can alienate and isolate them even further from each other. No one seems able to break the spell of "putting it behind them" and sadly, they suffer in silence rather than support and lean on each other. Perhaps it will change over time.

Feeling Lost

Dante knew the the sheer hopelessness that can grip us when he wrote:

"In the middle of the journey of our life I found myself within a dark wood where the way was wholly lost."

Losing someone close, there is not only the loss itself to contend with, there can also be the feeling of being lost, sometimes disoriented for a long time afterwards. Daily life is strange because all the usual ways of thinking and doing things are not right anymore. Routines and habits of living are skewed and empty since they no longer involve our loved-one, just a reminder of their absence. Then in the spur of the moment that can be forgotten, just for a while. Until a confrontation comes with the reality—again. The moment of truth, over and over. They are gone, forever. It is mystifying.

Like the caterpillar going into the chrysalis, there is no instruction manual for this huge inner transition. We must rely on intuition and trust the body-heart-mind to find its way. We don't know yet how we will come out of this, but know we will. The caterpillar cannot predict how long it will be in the chrysalis, or in what form it will emerge. Grief is like that. We feel wholly lost. Then slowly, imperceptibly, a new form of our life emerges. Goethe put it beautifully:

> So long as you have not experienced this
>
> to die and so to grow
>
> you are only
>
> a troubled guest on the dark earth

Standing in the Fire

Looking from the threshold of fire over this experience, we can see our inner strength and the practices we found of not-knowing, bearing witness, and compassion, practices big or small that held us up through the most intense flames. Now we can take some time to nurture our scorched emotions, thoughts and hopes.

The intensity of grief when it first sets in can bring us to our knees. Sometimes we carry grief for many years. Grief leaves us dealing with its pervasive cloud that descends indiscriminately like a blanket over our life. We can try to push it to the back of mind, giving the impression that grief has been spent or resolved. Grief will run its course, and when ready, release us to the life we have still to lead. It takes its own time and cannot be hurried.

Standing in the Fire

When brought to your knees
by grief and vulnerability
that takes you into
the raw humility and
earth of your being

When you don't rush away
in fright or pain
but stand right in the fire
ready to burn;
Then to amazement

what burns is not the self
but the terrible fear,
the extraneous stuff
that feeds the false self
on the periphery of being.

When you pause after the fire
you descend earth-deep
to the roots of your ancestors
blessed and awed by all
that brought you to being

When you stay longer
in a sacred state
to join the underground river,
the river of shared meaning,
you find humanity at its best

Then
with almost unbearable
love and calm
you are taken
immersed and bathed
in elusive and
infinite oneness.

Chapter 4

Rites of Passage

At this time, perhaps more than at any other in life, we need ceremony, ritual and rites of passage. A ceremony involves community and marks a significant event such as taking up a public office, a marriage or a funeral. A ritual can be individual or collective, is usually repetitive and provides structure, focus and meaning with an intent of continuity or assisting a practice, such as meditation or contemplation. A rite of passage is generally a longer process involving an individual arriving at a life-intersection; it involves introspection and a trial or ordeal to undergo with increased self-knowledge as the best result. The rite of passage is a preparation for the next major stage of living, or at the end of life in preparation for dying. Ceremony, ritual and rites of passage share connection to the big transition points of living and dying.

Grief as a Rite of Passage

While the funeral is a ceremony, grief is a rite of passage. It focuses attention on the acknowledgement and initiation of the big life transitions, including moving to a life without your loved-one. The grief rite of passage provides an initiation into the change that lies ahead for you, that you will create. Initiations are shaped by an underlying archetypal pattern that calls for inner work—at the coming of age, and later in life, the seeking of wisdom, each call for a shift from the small, reactive self to a more expanded, magnanimous self. Healing and growth are particular desired outcomes of the rite of passage.

Grief is like this. It is a natural rite of passage that affects us personally and opens our heart and mind to new levels of insight to prepare for the next major stage in life: life without our loved-one and all it implies. Family and community used to play a significant role through a series of rituals to provide support, important witnessing, mentoring and comfort for those grieving. Sadly, community involvement is now missing from grief which is largely hidden away from view.

As the dying companion or the one close to the departed, the grieving passage serves to initiate us into life ahead without our loved-one. Grieving is such an embodied and powerful experience, the initiation happens with or without community support, and mostly these days it is a solo passage. We can make it a sacred passage, and once we have passed through it, be able to support others through their grief.

The Funeral: Friends Say Goodbye

There are many societies in the world today who treat death differently to our Western approach. There is grief but without fear and anxiety. Family and community are involved and death and dying are treated as a natural community process with a home-centred and hands-on experience. Family and friends come to visit the one dying to wish them well on the dying journey. It is the opportunity for the one dying to say their final words to relatives and special community members. An elder or leader might bestow certain powers to specific people and pass responsibilities on to them.

In places as far away from each other as Ireland and India,

families stay with the body for one or more days, often not leaving the departed alone. Family members gather round to say their goodbyes, remember the life of the departed and wish the soul well on its journey. In India, they take part in dousing the body, grooming the hair, anointing the body with fragrances, dressing the sheath with flowers, herbs and leaves, wraping and preparing the body for burial or cremation. Irish custom today still includes family anointing and laying out the body, viewing the body by family and friends who "pay their respects" and farewell the dead. Then they open the window for the spirit to leave, close the coffin, carry the coffin through the home streets, and after the funeral lower the coffin into the grave.

It is in contrast to what happens today in our society. It is the norm to die in a hospital, hospice or other facility rather than at home. Consequently, we may not be present when our loved-one dies, nor have any time with their body to say goodbye once they have gone. Is this where the Western death phobia has come from?

There are ways to say goodbye even years later (see the Chapter on Soulwork) and I am living proof. Spiritual teachers from many disciplines tell us the soul doesn't leave for one to three days or more after death. Medical scientists say they can't distinguish the exact time of death. This period of unknown gives us time to say our goodbyes in the hope it will be received by our loved-one.

Tasks to be attended to for the funeral can become personal rituals or ceremonies in the way they are carried out. Mindfulness brought to the approach and preparation of a task transforms it to a little ritual. Each of the tasks below entails symbolic ways to involve others on behalf of the departed:

Preparing music for the service

Curating a picture display

Designing an Order of Service

Delivering a eulogy and/or inviting comment

Ordering or preparing flowers

Choosing the pallbearers

Preparing music for the service

Favourite music says a great deal about the deceased and can bring back many memories of their life. Normally quiet and melodic pieces are chosen, sometimes with a happier or up-beat piece at the end if that is a good reflection of their personality. If they were not really interested in music, choose the music you like and ask others for their suggestions.

Curating the picture display

It is optional to have a medley of photos of the deceased, highlighting aspects of their life, either in a special section set to music, or running continuously through the funeral. You can involve family and friends by asking they contribute photos representing the loved-one's life and special memories. Usually the presiding celebrant or religious dignitary can help put this together a on computer if there is no one available to do it.

Designing an Order of Service

The Order of Service is more than its title suggests. More than just an outline of the service, it is a memento of the life of the deceased, often with a portrait image on the front. Included may be a short biography, funeral music named, and any explicit wishes, beliefs or special words of the departed highlighted. These are printed for all those attending the funeral to take away with them. The presiding celebrant or religious dignitary can help with the wording as needed.

Writing a eulogy

Eulogies are delivered by one or more people close to the deceased, such as close family members, a close friend or close professional associate. Eulogies can take many forms from a formal to a free-flowing speech. Here is an example in the form of a poem, written for an artist who died in the prime of life in sombre circumstances. He was found sitting alone on a garden bench one icy winter's morning. This poem was an adjunct to the main eulogy:

A Poem For Simon

How old was Simon? Most say mid-life
plenty of life left we thought. Plenty of time.
But life is like a double helix, two parts at once
best turns to worst, plenty to empty, time runs out.

Simon was loved by many, his art a mirror
reflecting dark nights when our soul is lost.
He chose to die in a silver-dew garden
a last manifesto to what life had been

with final defiance of friends and art
his soul returns to where it never left
and we send with it the most love we can give
… for Simon's soul, for Simon's garden art
for Simon

Inviting Comment

In addition, or as an alternative to a eulogy, consider inviting those attending the funeral who would like to make their own comment and offering about the departed, to step up. This enhances community feeling and gives those who do not have a formal role an opportunity to be part of the funeral ceremony. The presiding dignitary can facilitate this for you.

Ordering or preparing flowers

Flowers can symbolise much about your loved-one, for instance all one colour or one type of flower. Some people just have one single bunch of flowers and ask everyone not to send flowers but to make a donation to a particular charity, for instance the research arm of the hospital that treated them. Another option is to have the full bouquet of flowers covering the coffin and when the flowers are taken off the coffin after the service, invite everyone to take some home.

Choosing the pallbearers

There are six pallbearers to carry the coffin after the funeral. This can require diplomacy if you have more than six men and women who need some recognition and a role, or if it means that just one or two get left out. A wooden coffin with an adult body can be heavy even for six men, so choose those who are well able, or request the coffin is supported by a trolly. The presiding dignitary will instruct the pallbearers on what to do on the day.

The Day of the Funeral

After the death, the funeral ceremony becomes the single pivotal event for those closest, one that consumes thoughts and waking focus. There are many decisions to be made and details to attend to: arrangements for the body, burial or cremation; contacting the funeral parlour; choosing a coffin; notifying people; choosing a celebrant or religious person for the funeral; the style and format of the funeral or memorial service; compiling photos; catering and guest refreshments if there is a wake; flowers; eulogies; pallbearers; delegating tasks and managing the finances.

> I found nights sleepless and troubled. The strangeness and overwhelm of loss was mixed with the organisation of all the funeral tasks with people to consider, careful not to exclude anyone close. It was two weeks after his death until the funeral as we waited for family to return from overseas. The long hours and days passed slowly. Nights took forever. Then, with feelings of both dread and relief, the funeral day arrived.

Nothing prepared me for the confrontation of seeing the coffin knowing it held Martin's body and I became short of breath and thought I would faint. The finality of the funeral ceremony hit home at a deep gut level. A "celebration of his life" seemed a wistful refrain that just wasn't appropriate and was not mentioned. Even sitting through the photo medley of his life I found a stark reminder of his absence. Seeing the hearse slowly roll out into the road, then drive away felt unendurable.

The wake or reception entailed a flurry of people to greet who wanted to share their condolences. I tried to remember all their names through the fog of shock and grief and thank them for attending. Some were also upset. Eventually, many hours later, I finally found myself alone at the end of that long day, one never to be forgotten or repeated.

All these traditions seem heart-wrenching, yet they are a part of the public goodbye process. In other counties still more connected to the earth, the funeral is more participatory and confronting, sometimes witnessing the burning at the funeral pyre. In the Hindu religion the cremation happens usually within twenty-four hours of death, to free the soul from the body. In our society, the absence of touching the dead and our hands-off funeral customs stand in place of what was a basic, earthy function for family as part of letting go. The funeral left me totally unhinged, but the mistake is to regard it as something of comfort because that comes over time.

Fear of Funerals

Funerals have a powerful effect on those closest attending. Increasingly there has been a trend for a memorial service where the coffin is not present, and some humans have never been to a funeral with the coffin there, let alone seen an open coffin with the body on view. The distancing and hiding of death seems to add to the fear of death, now named as death phobia in Western societies. Apart from the avoidance of death and dying, death phobia can negatively affect others. A dying companion who sat with his mother to the last breath wanted his family to have an option to view the body and say goodbye, but his two siblings vetoed it, leaving all others sad and lacking completion.

What does it take to get back in touch with dying as a natural and beautiful ending of life? It could be part of life again, so there is not a great divide between the living, the dying and the dead. We can learn from how other societies do it. Instead of staying away from dying and loss we can embrace it, staying with our loved ones during their dying time, becoming a dying companion to them with their welcome, and approaching the dying process as a natural and intimately beautiful part of relationship.

Your Personal Rituals

Holding your own grieving rituals at home or privately in nature can be soothing and meaningful. Rituals are purposeful, structured actions that symbolise thoughts, emotional expressions, wishes and beliefs in relation to the death of our loved-one that set things to rest.

Rituals can be simple and small yet have big meaning. Here are some ideas:

Lighting a candle at a certain time of the day to remember your loved-one.

Placing flowers in a special part of your home.

Playing music that has meaning for you.

Reading a poem out loud or saying something special for your loved-one.

Calling someone close to your loved-one every month for the first year.

The important thing is setting your intent beforehand. Clear the space literally and psychologically, so that you have uninterrupted time for the ritual. Have a sequence in mind. Work out the things you need. Get these things ready before starting. Clearly mark the start and end of the ritual, for example, with music or by lighting and then extinguishing a candle. More ideas for personal rituals can be found in IV: Ritual and Contemplation.

The Soulful Garden

After my husband died I spent a year alone on our farm before I sold it and had to leave. Neighbours, friends and family, especially my daughter and step-son, were kind, caring and respectful of my solitude. Days alone in my big garden were painfully sad, beautiful and reflective. I loved the garden. I grew it, worked it and wrote poetry there.

The garden is a metaphor for the soul. It is universal, reaching across cultures, time and space, beyond the personal to a sense of the collective. The 'Beautiful Endings Poem' is about the garden or a special place you shared with your own loved-one, a real or metaphorical place you now must leave or that will never be the same without them. I wrote the poem with those of you in mind who would one day read it.

Beautiful Endings Poem

As your days in this place
draw to a close
you see beauty everywhere
in the garden that you
planted and grew.

Absorbed
you want to take in
every moment
as though the whole world
is speaking to you.

We constantly meet
the little endings
like the loved pair of shoes
that can't be repaired
just one more time

and sadly we discard them.
All practice runs
for the Grand Endings
we each must face.

It seems simple enough
the ending itself
has its own beauty

and like a forgotten glimpse
of the holy grail
the world lights up
with a hundred bird songs.

This chapter is done.
And if you listen
the whole world
is speaking to you.

II | Grieving as Sacred Process

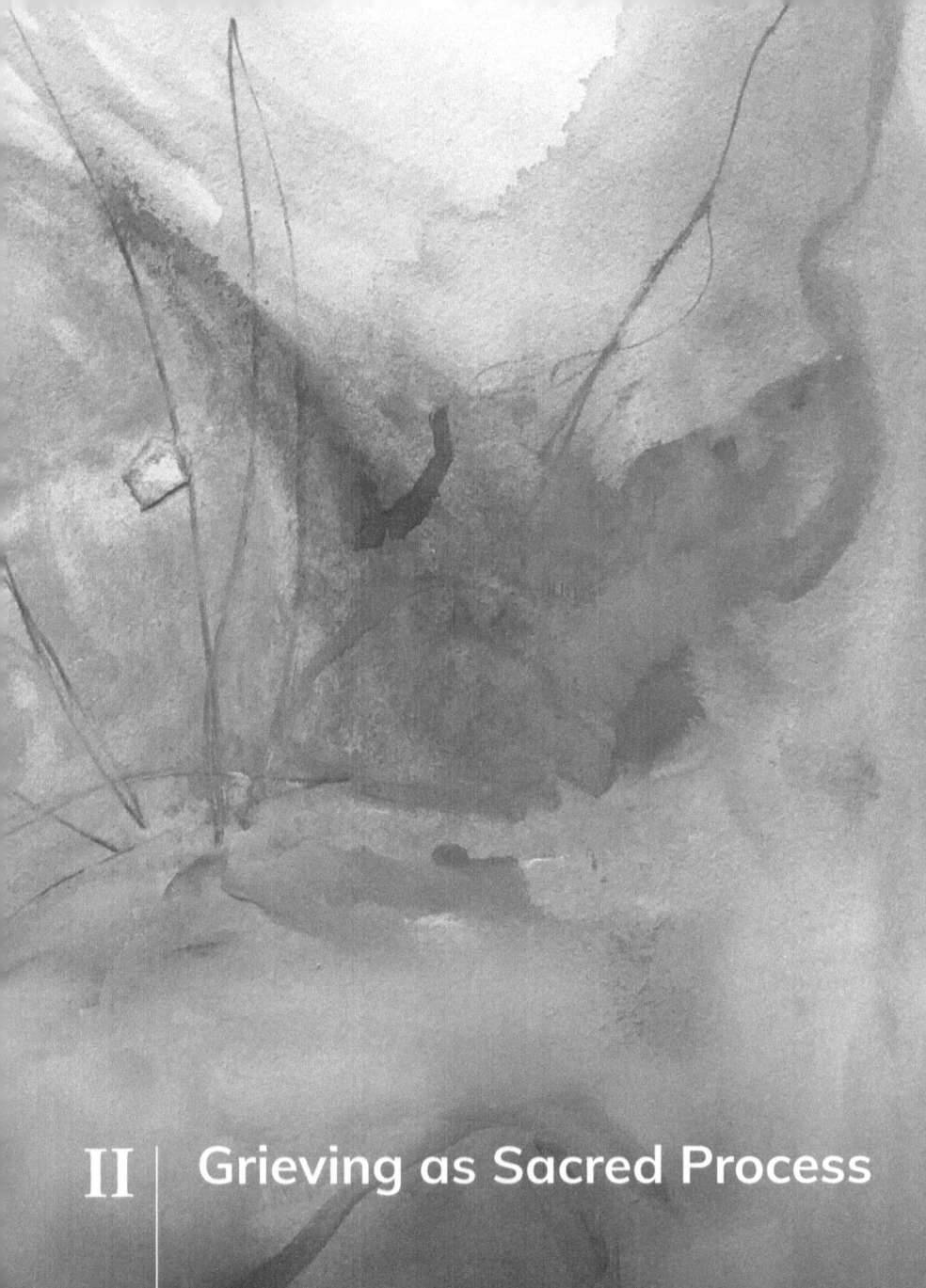

The Second Threshold: *Pilgrimage*

The task of the second threshold, Pilgrimage, is to grieve as sacred process. Grief is a transformational space and one we undertake essentially on our own, even when others are close. Everyone will experience grief at some stage in life. Like any sacred process, it puts us in touch with our soul as long as we don't block the connection. A descent to the deep lands of grief can be met, and we are encouraged go fully into the territory of grieving knowing that after the descent comes an ascent. Grieving has been described by mythologist and author, Michael Meade, as the deepest emotion. Grief is also the natural healing process for great loss.

Looking back two years after the death of my husband I see my grief was like a pilgrimage. It is a sacred process. A pilgrimage doesn't have to be a literal journey of going on a long walk to a significant destination (although at first that is precisely what I did and took small groups to walk forests and ocean lands together in reflective silence). With a pilgrimage we expect a way forward, but the true way is inward.

A pilgrimage is a passage of spiritual significance and a private journey to our inner world. A pilgrim walks a physical path with their own motivation, but tend to share some outcomes such as animating and magnifying the inner heart-mind-soul landscape.

During the inner pilgrimage of grief, images and insight from the soul arise as we walk (or even waltz as Irish women are prone to do) through the most sacred inner realms. Oscar Wilde knew this when he wrote in *De Profundis*:

"Where there is sorrow there is holy ground."

Taking on pilgrimage as a metaphor has proven helpful to grieving. It's a path with a start and an ending, for one thing, and that's a relief because grief can feel as though there may never be an end to it. As a grief pilgrim, we continuously choose whether to be with others or to be alone; and social expectations lose significance as we are guided by what we need and the powerful embodiment of grief. We decide to join conversations, listen silently or be alone. To go to the depths of our grief is spiritual, not necessarily religious, yet a sacred process. Grief requires solitude and quiet, which is what we encounter as a pilgrim and what many people naturally seek while grieving. Even those who do not follow a religion can be found in places of worship for the tranquility and solace offered there. We can claim that quiet space in our homes too.

We go on a pilgrimage for our own reasons and share some things in common: a pilgrim travels in a way different to other travellers. A pilgrim travels slowly, often walking much of the way so time and physical effort are involved; a pilgrim travels consciously, closely observing the self as well as the terrain and other humans they meet; a pilgrim spends time in contemplation; and they seek development, deepening, an answer or some form of inner change as an outcome of the journey. All that sounds like what is needed for a loving and restorative grieving journey.

Sacred Message

With fire burning inside your heart
you face an impossible truth
while all the noise fades
as silence greets you
and everything
you knew is
not there
no life
left.
How
can you
stop your
fall into that
well of darkness
and grief so black
there is no way out?
But wait. There is a small
foothold and if you look up
a sunset of fire and beauty holds
the symbol of some sacred message.

Chapter 5

The Person is Gone: Your Relationship Continues

As the shock subsides the heartbreak lingers. This chapter, The Person is Gone, is an invitation to consider that the relationship continues with our loved-one. It continues internally, in what goes on in our thoughts and heart. Sometimes there are surprising reactions with incidents from long ago being remembered again, incidents that still hold wonderful or difficult emotions. This is your time now. You no longer are the dying companion. It is over. You are freed from the responsibilities of being the loving witness. That time has passed.

While logic defies, it is normal to wonder where our loved-one has gone. Or when we're alone, to talk to them as though they are here in the room with us, or beside us out walking. These are aspects of coming to terms with the shock and reality of the loss. Eventually it will pass and fade gradually and naturally. It takes time to accept the seeming impossibility of our loved-one being gone permanently.

Strange thoughts and behaviour are often part of grieving. It is not the time to be harsh with yourself by exercising the inner critic. It is not the time to scold yourself or be the severe judge, nor start telling yourself you must be an idiot to think such crazy things. The rational part of our mind can extend kindness as well as logic and assessment, and be there to aid us. Be gentle with yourself. Keep hold of some humour whenever you can. Let your body and intuition tell you what is needed for grieving. As in a literal pilgrimage, sometimes the destination of grief surprises us.

Touching a Part of Heaven

Once someone you love dies, the memory of your relationship together can start to feel like it was special, outstanding. Reminiscing about the good times might seem like they were heaven. When we have touched a part of heaven, we pine for heaven to return. Characteristic of this time, especially early on, is idealising the loved-one and the life we shared with them. More and more, we look at our lost life with them as special and dearly missed, and skip over the ordinary bits and irritations. Nevertheless, feeling as though we have lost a bit of heaven may persist and with it comes a certain and rare kind of loneliness; pining. We know our pain cannot be eased by anything in the external world.

The way out is to go in. The more we become in touch with our inner world and deep time, the more we are able to go through and out the other side of our lamentations. When we face and bear the reality, the banal and more negative aspects of the relationship with the loved-one can be recalled too. This brings some balance and perspective. It doesn't mean we love them any the less, perhaps the opposite, and is a bearable diversion from the heaven ideal. It becomes a restorative process as we reclaim a deep connection with the whole of our relationship in all its humanity.

Grief is strange. Grieving isn't always a matter of sorrowful and loving memories of our loved-one and the fond times shared, which is hard enough. This chapter looks at broader concerns. Sometimes unexpected feelings erupt. We are human and relationships have strong and weak terrains, good and bad times, personal regrets — and we are left with them as our relationship lingers on. Unresolved difficult emotions live on as well. Unsettled and negative emotions in grief are what seem to cause the most unhappiness and distress. Carrying the weight of incidents, hurts and blame, with words said and regretted, wounds suffered in silence or thoughts never spoken, the leftover emotions will continue on into our future. An alternative to denying or suffering these relational aspects, is to start releasing them now and clear the weight we carry. Once we have some clearing and a sense of what belongs in the past that can be laid to rest, we have room to breathe again.

Following are stories of difficult emotions and grief reactions. Only a few examples are covered and there are many others, some more serious and wounding than these. This chapter is the darkest in the book and was the hardest to write. I have included it to show many emotions can come up during grief including those we would rather not feel, and it is far better to acknowledge them than try to ignore them.

Recognition

Emotions are intensified during grief; we can acknowledge and recognise this as well as emotions that arise after we do not want to feel.

> Marion loved her father and was glad to look after him when he became ill with cancer. After Marion's mother died, they were the only family left. Now her dad had died she was trying to understand why she felt bitter, and guilty for feeling so bitter.
>
> Emptiness and longing for the old life with her dad stirred

up a flood of feelings. She began to feel negative and bogged down by grief, on a path that took her away from where she wanted to be. Marion tried some pretty big changes; a new lover, a holiday. Something more was needed beside a change.

Marion recounted a dream she had that summed it up for her: "I was leading a project, it was important and very exciting. Then I arrived one day to find they locked me out of my office. No one knew anything about it, except some higher authority had done it. I became increasingly frantic and furious. I couldn't get access to my computer and material. Through a window I could see my phone had also gone. Stolen. I was stopped dead, locked out, unable to function. I was so frustrated and helpless. It's actually exactly the way I feel now that my father is gone. I'm locked out and frustrated. I feel guilty about it. I was happy to look after him even though it took me away from work and I missed out on important things.

"Lying in bed mulling over the dream I had an amazing insight—no one is locking me out except myself. It is me! And as I thought about that over the next few weeks, I began to see how I did it to myself. And the amazing thing? If I was doing it, that meant I could stop it!"

It takes courage for that step of recognition and responsibility. Marion had been at the edge for months since the funeral. Then she found an opening, a way to take some steps forward. Making emotional sense of being bitter, and then guilty for such an unwanted emotion, was the move toward being accountable for them. We can't rely on logic and reason to make "emotional sense"; I know people bitter and angry at the one dead because their loved-one abandoned them by dying. Fear often resides underneath anger, but it is difficult to uncover because anger is defensive and often judgemental and righteous.

Negativity compounds grief and makes it worse because, if we are needing resolution with our lost loved-one, with bitterness and anger present it is unresolvable. Sometimes we have no choice but to attend to emotions due to the strength of them.

Grief Avoidances and Responses

Grief is hard work. We say goodbye to someone we don't want to part with, goodbye to the part of us that belongs with them and the relationship, and goodbye to an era in our life. No wonder we might try to avoid such broken heartedness. As promised in the Introduction, here are some of the usual attempts to avoid grief and try to protect against suffering, but all have consequences:

Become armoured. We try to close ourselves off to protect our sense of fragility, vulnerability and the fear of bottomless grief. The consequence is the enjoyable feelings that sustain us become armoured too and are not transmitted out nor are others good feelings able to get through.

Act like a victim. This is not the same as leaning on someone for a while. It is convincing our selves that we are not able to stand up on our own. It is not true and leads to dependency, a loss of self-determination and a gain in self-doubt.

Find an escape route. Distract ourselves with entertainment, travel, getting fit, diet, work, or find something that takes over life, like a cause or a big task, so that we never have to think about the ending that has just changed our life forever. The consequence is the grief doesn't go away, it gets buried within, eventually contaminating our lives.

Reactions like these rob us of grieving as sacred process. Luckily, they are reversible as long as we recognise and take responsibility for our avoidance reaction. None of them are worthy of who we really are, nor the living we have yet to do. I see them as old patterns of protection and survival from childhood that diminish who we are and come about because we don't know what else to do, or we are not paying attention and go along with an automatic reaction. Many patterns from the past belong in the past—we invented them because they worked in the context and situation back then but, if they no longer serve us, need to change. Reactions are habitual, repetitive or impulsive; responses are mindful, considered, and growthful. For more specifics, see Ritual and Contemplation and The Person is Gone: Your Relationship Continues

Grief Responses

How do we stand such suffering? No wonder we try to turn our back on grief by denial, postponing or fighting it. Yet there is nothing to fight, and anyway, fighting to supress grief does not work. Grieving is a solo pilgrimage that cannot be completed alone and talking to others grieving can help us grieve. A few people talking together about facing fears and grief is an enormous relief that makes suffering bearable.

To surrender to grief is to rise above the fear of suffering. Then a door opens to meaning and solace.

Abuse

This is a sorry story of abuse and control during the last years of life, probably due to the onset of dementia. Dementia can creep up and affect people in different ways, at times bringing out long-abandoned traits, defences or reactions from childhood experiences. The focus of the story is the carer who was the abused in this case. It is not for the faint-hearted.

> Jorge became increasingly angry toward Alicia, his wife, during his last six years of life. This was always in private, although he gradually started treating her disparagingly in company too, pointing out her faults in the third person when she was right beside him, as though it was his right or a joke. At first she objected, but got such an intimidating tongue-

lashing when they got home that soon she said nothing.

As time went on, Jorge became more verbally abusive when they were alone, reducing Alicia to tears. Then he would ignore her for days. The abuse was frightening enough, but then he started making threats to her life as well. Alicia was living a life of fear and dread as she became increasingly isolated and controlled. All this was undetectable to others. Her only explanation was it was some kind of dementia. When an aggressive cancer was diagnosed giving Jorge just months to live, he started an intensive regime of treatment and relied heavily on Alicia as his carer. His attitude toward her changed, probably brought on by shock, his vulnerability and the large doses of drugs, and Jorge became loving and respectful toward Alicia once again. He died nine weeks after the diagnosis.

Alicia was left feeling grateful. She had the real Jorge back at the end, although could not forget being abused, frightened and wounded over the six years beforehand. Her grief was prolonged over many years, a mix of sorrow, confusion and relief that she was released from the dreadful deterioration of her life. She resolved to keep it secret from family and friends and told herself his abuse was dementia at work and not really Jorge feeling disdain and hate for her. She was glad of the last nine weeks they had together and regarded them as a time of forgiveness and being reunited.

After circumstances and ordeals as difficult as this, grief is a grim pilgrimage to set out on. However hard and complex the relationship and your emotions, grief is a time you can resolve them. Human relationships are not always good or healthy and can leave a lasting impact on the rest of life. There are ways to resolve even the most testing relationship after someone dies, and when deep-seated wounding and fear were involved, I encourage you to seek professional guidance. Some things are just too hard to do alone.

The Unlived Life

This story is for you if you feel as though part of your life was taken away from you, possibly while being a carer or possibly through other circumstances or choices you made. The unlived life is a one you feel you have forgone but would have loved and are left with regret. Grief can surface things we may have carried for a long time as we see in this story of Pauline.

Until Bill died, Pauline was his primary carer. How could she not be? Bill was her soulmate. It meant her life was interrupted and derailed, but it seemed a small price to pay. Two big projects she was pursuing had to go on hold along with the weekend sport she loved, but at least she could keep her job.

At first it was an interim arrangement, just until Bill got better. As the months went by, it became apparent that Bill was not going to get better. It turned out that what started as part-time care escalated into full-time care. Pauline did it willingly. She loved Bill. But somewhere in the back of her mind, frustration and resentment had grown.

Pauline had two work projects and they would have been the crowning glory of her career, opening new doors. In her absence, the boss gave them over to a workmate who would get all the accolades. Pauline fretted for her staff as well as the projects, seeing both as having slipped through her fingers. Over time her frustration became so much she smashed some china one day at home in private. Resentment crept into her care for Bill. "It's a betrayal to admit these negative things, even privately. I have such a good relationship with Bill. I'm being selfish and indulgent to think about myself and getting on with my own life. I should be thinking of him. If the tables were turned, and I was the one who was sick, he'd be completely there for me. I'd be devastated to think Bill resented me."

Guilt welled up. Logic told Pauline that circumstances had overtaken her. It was no one's fault. Yet in her private moments she became more resentful of her position and of her workmate. Pauline thought she was becoming a monster and pushed such thoughts away, pushed them down to where they came from. But she couldn't help but daydream... if only she were not in this predicament, if she was not tied down like this, imagine everything she would be doing! This was Pauline's time of life to shine, to do what she had always dreamed of. "But I've missed out. Missed the boat. It's too late now for me"

By the time Bill died ten months later, Pauline was quite a wreck, crying at night and snapping at people most of the day. People irritated her. Afterwards she was ashamed. It was not her normal self. The funeral was coming up and Pauline put her irritation down to the stress of it all. Things would change after the funeral was over.

The funeral came and went, but Pauline's resentment stayed on. The weeks went past. Her sister suggested that she needed a holiday. That would make all the difference and put an end to her stress, wouldn't it?

If you identify with Pauline's predicament, read on with some compassion for yourself. Don't underestimate the impact of being the companion and bearing witness to your loved-one's dying.

Thoughts of an unlived life can take hold as it did with Pauline, shake you to the bone and haunt your nights. Dig deep and you may find the thoughts are fear-based and come from a mindset of scarcity: for instance, Pauline thinking that such a good opportunity will never come again. If we allow these thoughts to colonise us it leads to symptoms. Physiologically, our muscles tense and contract ready for fight, freeze or flight, leading to symptoms like tension headaches and sleepless nights. Psychologically, our world contracts as fear-based thoughts continue, which can bring up defensive feelings like anger, resentment and blame. With a contracted view, the available options seem to shrink and a vicious cycle of thought forms.

After being caught in some situations where I felt blocked, the following realisation dawned on me:

The unlived life does not lie behind us. It lies ahead.

As long as we investigate what is at its essence, for that is what the soul is really seeking, we can build the essence of a longed-for unlived life into our future.

> Pauline eventually forgave the missed opportunity, forgave herself and her bitterness and let go attachment to what she felt entitled to and had missed out on. These were the cards life had dealt. A year later she found a new path for herself. It was in a much smaller family firm that meant taking a drop in pay, but she was given trust and full responsibility. More importantly, Pauline was attracted to the people, their ethos and the fact that she was the eldest in the firm. She flourished and became like a mentor to the others — a role she loved that stayed with her for the rest of her life.

Grief may be what we don't expect and may not be all sorrow. Unusual and strong emotions are part of grief and preside until it runs its course. We can help the emotion lose its grip by acknowledging it rather than by pretending it isn't there. Trying to repress and control isn't effective as the unwanted emotion leaks out sooner or later. Emotional work needs to be cleared to avoid projecting it where it has no place and harms relationships.

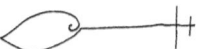

We return to the unlived life to investigate it further in Part III, Living Without Them; see the chapter titled Silken Threads. Forgiveness is explored in the next chapter on Soulwork. Rituals to help in Part IV are Grounding Meditation, On Gratitude, and

Self-Forgiveness.

To look more closely at underlying emotions of guilt, shame, anger, fear and entitlement, they are set out in Part IV: Ritual and Contemplation, starting with Practice 15, The Person is Gone: Your Relationship Continues, through to Practice 20, a Contemplation on Entitlement.

Overwhelm

When it all feels too much, pause. Find a quiet place. It need not be far; outside in fresh air is best. When I was in the hospital every day I went to sit on a couch in a corner of the corridor for five minute breathers and notice what was going on around me. Back home after he died, I went outside into our big garden.

Notice the sounds, see the colours, if there's a window see the sunshine, the raindrops, or go outside and feel the breeze on your face, literally smell the roses, and see the effect of the wind in the trees. Just these small things help to revitalise. See IV: Ritual and Contemplation, Burnout and Overwhelm.

Alone and All One

On the path alone
like a pilgrim
your loved one gone
in a wisp of wind

leaving silver stars and
clouds on the moon
all one behind you
now reflected here
in dark waters ahead
with little frogs
and fireflies

Walk toward
a gold horizon
not the one
you see with
rainbow promise
but your soul's
horizon nestled
within.

Chapter 6

Soulwork

After being there so fully for others throughout the dying time—maybe you were a dying companion, maybe you organised the funeral and all that goes with the estate—sooner or later it is time to tend to your self. At the threshold of pilgrimage, now in the absence of our loved-one, we are at the start of an inner passage that provides time to more fully attend to what is going on for us and make meaning of it all. If you want to grow, this isn't just an option. Our grief demands it of us.

Grief opens us out, as though our whole chest is pried apart, heart, gut and soul laid bare. There is a physicality to grief that engulfs and dominates, making us entirely vulnerable to its whim. Too often we try to stop the grief, to ease its force, cover it over, and soldier on. This is like trying to stop the flow of a waterfall. It can be done, by being damed up. We all know the consequences; eventually there will be an overflow or burst out. In putting attention and energy into minimising and damming up grief, we miss its gift. We miss the sacred pilgrimage and being transcendent.

The work of contemplation comes naturally to grieving. Contemplative work and inner learning are part of spiritual traditions the world over. It is called by many names such as the journey to enlightenment, higher consciousness, oneness, self-transcendence, illumination, revelation, consciousness evolution, and spiritual awakening. This work goes deeper than emotions with a greater truth than the mind alone. It is the work of the soul, both a descent and a refuge. To know light we must know dark. Some say we can go up only as far as we have gone down: if we refuse to feel the full depth of our grief we cannot feel the full height of our joy.

Soulwork is inner work, the work of the psyche. The word psyche is from the Ancient Greek *psykhe* meaning "the soul, mind, spirit; one's life, the invisible animating principle". It is the animating inner-work we do to restore our self, to reconnect with our soul. Make no mistake, soulwork is work just as taxing and rewarding as any meaningful and creative work you might do in the outer world. Part of soulwork is the resolution of negative and troubling emotions. The resolution is rarely if ever found in the external world, such as blaming others or going away on a holiday. That is like looking for your keys under a streetlight when you dropped them inside! Resolution is found within.

Looking outside our selves can blind us to what is inside. An example is to see aggression in your family or friend, but be oblivious to the aggression in yourself. Of course what we see in others runs the full range of human experience, and so can be anything from aggression to hubris, timidity or betrayal. Although the psychological concept is modern, ancient texts warn us of it, such as the well-know verse from the Bible that cautions, "Hypocrite—first take the log out of your own eye, then you will see clearly enough to remove the spec from your friend's eye." In Jungian psychoanalytic terms this is the shadow side at work, a side of our selves that keeps us from self-knowledge and growth. The book I write next will be on developing consciousness and harvesting life, where I take the reader on a deep dive into the shadow, including positive qualities of our own that we don't acknowledge and project out onto others.

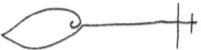

Soulwork is private work. In Part IV I show you some contemplative methods, rituals and journaling for your own enquiry and exploration. Some trusted guides along the way are useful to clarify, stimulate and sort the stuff that we carry with us internally, to clear the mind and become more insightful and whole. This work is like opening the third eye—once opened, we can't avoid reflecting on the meaning of what we see.

The invitation is to descend into grief. It takes time to sort who we are now in life given the change to a greater or lesser extent without our loved-one and the dynamic role with them (parent, spouse, child, or friend). This is not the same as making a plan for the future. Looking to the future has its place to inspire direction, effort and encourage setting goals. We learn this through projects, commitments such as raising a child, and skill-mastery. Equally, the future can be used as a way to avoid the present and avoid being still, within our self. With time, stillness and the help of some practices, we can arrive at a deep knowing within about the rhythm of life now. With heartbreak comes a deeper level of truth.

Work of the Soul

'Work is love made visible'
those beautiful words
of Kahlil Gibran
writing from the heart

or digging garden dirt
with sun and rain
growing something
beyond yourself

work to express "I am"
a gift to those you love
giving voice to your
soul's lost symphony.

Soulwork Is Not Wallowing

Soulwork is not wallowing. With wallowing there is a want to stay inside our misery as though it is some kind of safe refuge or where we now belong. Wallowing is self-indulgent complacency, which has its appeal from time to time, and can take over unless we wake up. In contrast, soulwork is active, aware and conscious. It is made of contemplation, inquiry, observation, compassion and discernment. Soulwork rises well clear of narcissism and is not to be confused with self-indulgence.

Self-observation without judgement is a powerful spiritual pathway. Viktor Frankl, the esteemed psychiatrist and Holocaust survivor, encourages us to notice the space between a stimulus and our response. He claimed it is this space in between that distinguishes a conditioned reaction (like Pavlov's dog) from a response. In the space we have choice, when we are aware. If we practice at consciously lengthening the space between, we become clearer, more creative, more free.

On a practical side, here is a fivefold approach to the outcomes that come from soulwork:

Self-observation and developing a capacity to bear witness— like the "Zen observer", remaining clear and unentangled without losing compassion.

Unlearning false assumptions and defences accumulated over the years. In so doing we become more aware and develop an awareness of our awareness.

Understanding and accepting that life is a mix of pleasure and pain that is not controllable.

Embodying being at peace with life as it is and ceasing to wish for something else or caught in magical thinking, a belief that wishing for something will make it materialise.

Making your wholehearted contribution to others and to life, for this is your part in the whole to enhance the world by the gift that only you can give.

Soulwork Themes and Approaches

In the next sections we take a brief look at themes of soulwork relating to grief in order to demonstrate the nature of the exploration you can do. The work of the soul is not literal, it is by definition metaphorical and symbolic and I have tried to make it as accessible as possible.

Approaches used to enter into soulwork are described here. Themes in this chapter include non-attachment, the inner-witness, humility, forgiveness and gratitude. The importance of the last goodbye, which can be done even years later, is demonstrated in a story. More specific detail and techniques such as Soulwork Journalling and Grounding Meditation can be found in section IV: Ritual and Contemplation.

Dying and Inner Truth

Because dying is a heightened spiritual time, inner truth and speaking our truth become more significant and a way of seeking closure. As Euripides put it, "A circle gently closes." We know implicitly when that happens.

We are born with two aspects or realms of our self. Like yin and yang, together they form a whole. One aspect serves all we need to do to live in the world and advance society—our reasoning, logic, goal-setting, labour, enterprise—everything that enables us to practically look after ourselves and our families, to build structures, advance technologies, make judgements and reach conclusions. This realm dominates our society. The other realm is of the soul; it is love, spiritual intelligence and self-transcendence, together with deep body-mind knowing. Generally, these two realms become separated during living as we manage day to day of life, one realm being lost or overshadowed by the other.

Accompanying a loved-one on their dying passage tends to bring forward the lesser-known realm of the soul. It bears a most beautiful and spiritually courageous gift to our loved-one when they are able to receive it. The gift is our innate wisdom and inner beauty.

Inner Resources

Everyone has resources within to face the dying and death of their loved-one. We are so much more than what we think we are, with layer upon layer of life experience, depth and meaning. We just need to know when to reach for, and trust, our inner resources rather than reach for an external resource. Relying on external resources can be a matter of habit, to go to someone we believe is wiser than we are, for instance. Then we can be swayed by their opinion which may run counter to our path. No one knows our own soul and feels the rising of our spirit like we do our selves. There are some times we are left with no choice, because there is not anyone to ask for help or we do not know what we need and therefore what to ask for. During the times we are thrown back on our own resources, it is possible to gain the best insight and take the biggest steps in the right direction. Those times give us faith in our self and teach us to listen and see the signs the soul sends.

In order to accompany a loved-one through their dying passage we partook of something deep from the heart. It called on our inner strength and magnanimity. Being a dying companion is as demanding as it is precious. Bearing loving witness, walking beside them and now facing their loss and absence, all takes its toll. Now we need care and attention.

The best and most immediate care and attention is from yourself.

It is a big adjustment to the loved-one's absence, a time of release and contemplation to restore what is good for our soul and will revitalise the spirit. Soulwork is depth contemplation, helped by ritual. It is knowing we will heal, remembering treasured times as well as regrets. Soulwork is a way to consciously heal.

Gratitude

Gratitude and grief go together like yin and yang. Gratitude and grief need each other. Gratitude gives balance to grief and soothes or quickens healing. A little pocket of the day devoted to gratitude became a practice that saved me at the darkest times. Gratitude is considered by some as one of the highest forms of thought. It's a healthy emotion reminding us of all the good in people and in life and rebalancing time spent too long in lonely sorrow. All that is easy to forget as we enfold inward with grief. Gratitude teaches perspective and humility. Neuroscientists have studied the benefits of gratitude, and Professor Richard Davidson's studies at the Centre for Healthy Minds show gratitude increases positive mood, satisfaction, physical health, resiliency and decreases burnout. Interpersonally, gratitude strengthens relationships, community and group dynamics. Gratitude is a connecting force.

Deciding to be grateful is not sufficient alone, because it isn't only a mental activity. We must feel and embody gratitude through active appreciation and acknowledgment of what we value and are grateful for. We can practice gratitude through adopting a mindset of appreciation, acknowledging gratitude toward our fellow humans, community, and respecting our ancestors. In our grief, we can express gratitude for the special times with our loved-one and our life together. Imagine what we would have missed without them. Gratitude strengthens and brings joy.

We can regard grief itself as something to be grateful for. Grief brings intimacy and vulnerability to the centre of our experience. Grief could be seen as dead space, to get over a soon as possible; or as full of love and being alive. During times of grief we cut through the nonsense that has crept into life and go straight to what is real. Sometimes grief is prolonged. That's neither good nor bad, jus to be aware of. It can be held on to, as though it has become an old friend. This happens with a deeply buried belief that once grief subsides, all trace of the loved-one will disappear too, as if hanging on to the suffering and longing for them somehow keeps their memory alive. Therefore, suffering is maintained and stoked up rather than let die down to its natural embers.

Moving on from the intensive pain of grief takes us onto another grieving place. It is a place where the aching is overtaken by deep appreciation and gratitude for having shared our loved-one's life. Little by little, laughter returns as happy times are remembered and enjoyed again in memories. At first we don't believe it possible, but there comes a day when we remember without the stabbing pain. That deserves all the gratitude we can gather. Notes on Gratitude as a Practice can be found in Part IV.

Forgiveness

Forgiveness brings solace. After a time of punishing thoughts, forgiveness is like a graceful balm to soothe a troubled grieving mind. When it is self-forgiveness that is needed, a readiness to forgive others follows. Do what it takes to forgive and have mercy, that old-fashioned term.

Avoiding forgiveness is like dragging around a ball and chain of toxic emotion, be it burning resentment, blame, guilt or shame. When we forgive, we are freed of the shackles. The following story is a situation requiring forgiveness, where I felt I failed my husband when he was dying. I gave it a great deal of thought and reflection and came to forgive myself for the decision taken. Hand in hand, I accepted that nothing could take away the pain of the situation.

> I couldn't take him home. That was all he wanted and I failed him. The prospect was totally overwhelming to me. The hospital had no jurisdiction to hold him, but counselled against it in the strongest possible terms. Just the thought of it reduced me to tears and I don't cry easily, but my body and soul sent an overwhelming message—it is beyond me, I

would not cope. He was a big man at six foot five inches, and weighed twice my weight. How could I possibly look after him at home? We lived remotely and home nurses could not be found to live in and cover the intensive care needed. Physically and emotionally I couldn't care for him 24 hours a day, administer intravenous drips and drains (which I knew nothing about), nor deal with any anomaly or emergency. But all he wanted was to go home. I felt for him. It was not like me to not give it a go. By this stage I was rundown and fatigued—scared too—what if his death was laboured and painful? We'd be there alone and isolated. What if he needed oxygen or intravenous drugs I couldn't administer? It was all far, far too big, beyond me and beyond the bounds of responsible care. Even though he kept asking I remained clear and it broke my heart.

Dilemmas that can break hearts may arise in one form or another. As the one dying is our beloved, we want to do everything for them. Everything. We are vulnerable and opened out. There are times we must make choices that protect ourselves or others, as well as being the best choice we can make for our loved-one in the circumstances. Hurt and sorrow sometimes result. It is so important that self-forgiveness accompany such hard choices, to put self-blame to rest. Self-forgiveness was both an end and an opening to a deeper spiritual life.

Humility

The vulnerability of bearing witness throughout the dying time takes us into our humility. Humility for the gift of life itself, for humanity, for our own human nature. Humility is a powerful concept. The etymology of the word is from the Latin, humilis, which means humus—earth. The experience of humility takes us into the earth of our being. We return to the depths and roots of who we are. Humility grounds us.

Endings bring us face to face with non-permanence. As we face our loved-one's death, any delusions dissolve of something lasting forever or the ending being sometime in the future. When someone close who we love dearly is dying, we are confronted with the prospect of their total and sudden disappearance. Intellectually, it is likely you knew it was coming yet the full force sinks in once they have died. Practically, we can be left having to learn new skills and take on tasks that were previously done by our loved-one. In my case, neighbours who stepped up to help with running the farm was unexpected and touching. I knew they were the salt of the earth, but this was exceptional. It demonstrated the innate goodness in human beings and their kindness saved me from having to take more drastic measures, like a quick forced sale of the herd of cattle to deal with the situation.

It cannot be denied that endings are about many painful situations, decisions and the end of our world as we have known it. But in the midst of all that, there arises a certain clarity of vision. Clarity of the present moment, of what really matters. Clarity to see what is beautiful in life, even with all the faults and suffering.

Simultaneously as we grieve, we see the truth of who we are. It is not a false truth of spotlighting our failings, but the truth of our humanity and spirit. Many feel it as a huge weight of expectation lifted from their shoulders, or see it as the scales dropping from their eyes, as they discern what is most dear. It is humility in action, in balance. Humility brings us closer to our soul. Our truth.

The Inner Witness

The inner witness is a powerful inner resource that we harbour. It is using our powers of observation and staying neutral while viewing a specific situation and seeing our self in that situation. It is hearing what is being said without judgement or blame and watching the emotions we feel come and go. The inner witness appreciates the situation and is free from holding a fixed point of view, or taking sides during the action, jumping to conclusions or being rigid about an outcome. The inner witness is neutral and floats above the action.

We can call on our inner witness to review a past event and, as we get more proficient at it, to be available in the present moment when needed. It is like the part that comes to the fore when we bear witness for another, as described in Chapter 2. Now we bear witness to our self.

Try out being the inner witness. It takes practice. We watch our self and others as though we are looking through a camera lens. There is an awareness of the context we are in — the challenges, activity, people, sounds, smells, what we see and what we touch. From that point of view we also know what is going on internally, the difficult thoughts and emotions that arise, any fatigue we start to feel and concerns that occupy us.

The inner witness does not need to get involved in going over concerns, that is not its job. The inner witness has the capability to just hold everything. It is the part of us that can remain compassionate and detached with a calm mind, and the innate wisdom of the soul. Just to see the self and the situation from a different perspective is a relief and informs us of further options that could be taken, or reassures that it is all right, there is nothing to do except be present.

The inner witness is another way to embrace grieving by making meaning. I don't know if it's the same for you, but finding meaning in grief has been central for me. I'm still learning from the grief pilgrimage. Embracing meaning in grief is sacred and ennobles the spirit.

Non-attachment

Non-attachment is an important aspect of soulwork in grief and a way of gaining a grounded perspective on life and death.

As one of the concepts in Buddhist philosophy, non-attachment should not be confused with a lack of caring, feeling, commitment or with disregard. Care, love, commitment and regard all coexist with non-attachment. Rather, what non-attachment refers to is an absence of possession and a delusion of ownership of another. Non-attachment is understanding that things or others do not own you nor you them. It is easy to forget this when we feel attached. Through non-attachment in this way we promote respect, appreciation, acknowledgement, curiosity and sovereignty in relationship.

I thought a lot about impermanence and non-attachment during my husband's illness and after he died. I hoped a full understanding of non-attachment might bring calm and some peace. To my surprise, it helped, along with spiritual readings. Many spiritual teachers counsel that the notion of life and death is like a river, forever flowing, a beautiful analogy.

There was a distinct time my husband let go and surrendered to dying. I surrendered as well to the inevitable flow of his dying. We both put our trust in the dying process that was bigger than either of us. Despite whatever I wished or feared for myself, it was his time to leave this life and nothing either of us could do would stop it. I gave him all the reassurance I could that it was alright and he was doing his dying well, saying he was wrapped in love and light. After he died the only thing to do even in the darkest hours was to give my blessing and wish him well wherever he was, or if he was nowhere.

Non-attachment can be a difficult and harsh concept to grasp when you have lost someone you love, but the sooner I embraced it the better. Not to have done so would have exhausted my spirit, like trying to cling to the wind. We cannot hang onto things past their time. A Zen Master put it frankly to her student, "Everything breaks. Attachment is our unwillingness to face that reality."

Although it was Martin who died, a part of me died too. The

life we had together died. It is like the seasons. Afterward I felt as though it was winter when nothing grows, inside me as well as literally. It actually was winter at that time. All was bleak. But winter doesn't last; it's part of a cycle. Ever so slowly there is movement going on within, like all the growth we cannot see that happens underground before spring arrives and brings the new blooms.

Never Too Late to Say Goodbye

If you missed saying goodbye in the way you wanted, or think you have said goodbye but your loved-one's death or your regret still weighs heavily on you, then take heart. It is never too late to say goodbye and put your parting to rest. The following story is shared with you to demonstrate this, but there is a point of time to be aware of; it took place decades after the death. The story from my life demonstrates profound healing through a final goodbye and a lesson learned about perfection and love.

It all started when reading a book by the esteemed scholar and Buddhist teacher, Dr Jack Kornfield. I came across a line in the text that stood out above the others: "The point of dharma practice isn't to perfect yourself. It's to perfect your love".

How beautiful and simple are these words? Perfect your love. If only to remember them at the most crucial times! That is usually when my resolutions and hard-earned lessons fly out the window. To have the presence of mind to look through the lens of "perfecting your love" bypasses all the ego traps of defences and goes to the heart in a clear and profound way.

Unknotting things takes time and sometimes, just when you feel you've had enough and will never need to deal with it one more time – voila! There it is again. That is the magical time of soulwork when resolution and healing occur. Here is what happened.

Beyond Ghosts

Because my father died when he was eighty-four and I was eight, and because he had such long illness, I never knew him. We never engaged. Back in the late 1950s medical interventions were not all they are today. Wondering why he sired me at seventy-six, the only comment my mother ever made was, "All the young men were away at war. It was a terrible time." His reputation was of a proud, accomplished man-of-standing in the community with the mischief of the Irish. I suspect this well-dressed man, Tom, charmed and captivated my mother. Late in his career, his architectural practice was lost to a rogue partner; then he lost his health. Now that I am getting older myself I see how all that we regard as stable in life passes, and eighty-four is not nearly as old as I once thought it was.

As a little girl of eight years old, the image I had of my father was a sick old man spending long hours in the armchair in his room. I have no memory of him ever saying my name, of lifting me up or ever being a normal dad doing what dads do with their kids. Instead my father was gnarled and ancient, housebound, bad tempered and in a world of his own with a liking for weird food like sheep's brains in white sauce with onions.

Back then I knew he was in physical pain and I sensed his psychological pain. It was exacerbated by my much younger mother having to work to support the family, which both my mother and father saw as a disgrace. These facts had no language in my mind for their impact. But I watched. I could see. We tend to underestimate the capacity of children to grasp the meaning of existential issues going on around them. Here was my stranger-father, suffering and despairing. I hated having friends over to my house for fear they would see him and ask questions.

When my older brother and I played together, having fun,

there would be a tirade of anger toward me from my father, "Stop all that cussed laughing! Get out of my sight." Instantly I was reduced to tears, wounded to the core. I ran away to hide my shame for my father and for myself. I wanted to be loved but he could not express much to me except anger or indifference. Then my father died.

For a long time beforehand I knew it was coming. One night I could not sleep when I overheard the phone call to the doctor in the middle of the night, "We think the patient is dead." As an eight-year-old I wondered if I contributed to his death because I made him angry so much of the time.

In her hysterical state, my mother decided I was too young to go to the funeral and in truth she didn't want me there, so I was farmed out to relatives I didn't know for a month. I was disoriented, isolated and scared, but Aunt Jessie did her best to make me feel at home.

Sitting in her lounge room together, we looked at a painting on the wall of three horses galloping across a plain with a tense stormy sky behind. It was a stark but enthralling scene.

"We don't have a name for it yet. What would you call the painting?"

I looked deeply into that painting for a long time.

"Freedom."

Nightmares woke me in the dead of night with a fear of being haunted. It came from my Christian upbringing of life after death, which to my young mind meant ghosts. After trying to comfort my distraught mother by saying, "Don't worry mummy, you'll see him again in heaven," and her raging response, "Oh, don't be stupid, there's no such thing," I renounced religion then and there. With my father's death I decided that god was in the same category as Father Christmas and the tooth fairy and could be dismissed along with bible stories: teaching words spoken but not demonstrated.

The fear of ghosts and hauntings persisted.

As an adult, after many years reading psychological and philosophical texts, studying the human condition, having therapy on and off and being trained as a practicing therapist myself, I finally thought I had buried the father who haunted my mind. That part of my life was now resolved and dusted. I was free to get on with life and released from what stopped me from finding a way to be "perfect". If I could be perfect, even in a small way, then I would be loveable; I would be okay.

I was in my thirties and had been an adult from too early an age. My dream was to go to Esalen in California where the human potential gurus like Fritz Perls had built their practices. Once there, what awaited was a shocking surprise.

Esalen is situated on the majestic coast of Big Sur with natural hot springs on the cliffs looking out to the west over the Pacific Ocean. The place has abundant natural magic and power. During the morning of day one I felt a growing frustration with anyone in the group who was happy, including the group leaders. I didn't care how out of step this was and snapped, "We're here to work. I don't understand why you are laughing. There's nothing to laugh about."

We did a meditation together. Nothing unusual, focus on breathing . . . become present . . . relax the body. Soon sadness welled up in me like a rubber ball inflating within. Being an accomplished therapist, an independent single mum and a tough warrior, my tears astounded me.

What emerged as clear as crystal was an image of my father. Oh no, not again! I wanted to fight it and not go there. I'd done it all before and was finished with grieving. Yet in the spirit of being open to experience at Esalen, I went along with the images flowing in my mind to see what happened.

In my imagination, my dead father was laid out near naked in front of me on the earth, his thin concave self looking vulnerable like a withered child. After a time, I felt moved to pick up the small body of that wasted old man and, cradling him in my arms, turned and walked out over the beach at Big Sur. He felt light, like a featherweight. I waded out into the quiet ocean.

When I was waist deep in water, I paused and took in the moment. For some time I was just there, being, breathing the sea air, feeling the breeze on my face and the sand under my feet in cool waters, holding my father's body. Then gently I released my hold to let his body slowly float free on the calm sea.

As I watched, I wondered about Tom as a young man at my age, alive and full of energy with big dreams and a mission to fulfil. My age is the age he should have been as my father! But perhaps longing for the father he could have been is better than the real Tom would ever have been.

My next destination after the United States was his birthplace in Ireland. The anticipation gave me a profound feeling of spiritual connection, to him and to the place itself. I was to give a paper at Trinity College, Dublin, which is where Tom studied architecture, and it was to be the highlight of my trip, walking the same paths and corridors he walked. I had spent months in preparation trying to perfect the paper, trying to perfect myself.

In my vision, slowly, slowly the body drifted on the water and away to the west, toward the setting sun. Weeping, I threw fragrant rose petals after him and watched as his body was taken into the deep, until I could see no sign of it anymore and he was gone.

This vision, shared with the small group at Esalen, was a turning point in my life. It was finally to be the last goodbye. To my surprise, the ghosts were gone from my life from that time on.

The depth of love that I felt with that final goodbye to the father never known was deep as the teal ocean, as beautiful and sacred as the setting sun over the water.

Thirty years after that vision at Esalen, I have words that go to the heart of the experience with such clarity. Jack Kornfield's words. It's as though a trapdoor opened in my mind, dropping me down to a new level of meaning. Put simply, here is my insight:

No matter what I do to perfect my work, it misses the point of life and misses the point of my work, because that makes it about me, trying to perfect me. My work is for others, to heal and make a contribution and so be fulfilled. Jack Kornfield's words stay with me:

The point is not to perfect yourself . . .

The point is to perfect your love.

Chapter 7

Loneliness and Solitude

Loneliness is terrain long and hard to cross like a test of endurance. At times we want to give up, but we've come a long way along the path and the only viable option is to keep going. Remember there are other times the path takes us to beautiful places and we are touched with awe as the grief pilgrimage becomes sacred. Truly, grief is sacred all along. The descent into places of lament is accompanied by our soulwork and we find treasure in the dark to bring back on the ascent.

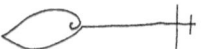

Loneliness is grim and bleak. Loneliness is suffering. We want to relieve it, to heal. Find a cure. We want to be free of the suffering that loneliness seems to impose and imprison us in. Regrettably, it goes on and on. We try all sorts of distractions but none work or bring only temporary relief. What to do? Will this go on forever?

Strangely, humans seem to perpetuate loneliness when in its grip, as though stuck there with glue. The glue is anxiety. Being lonely creates an anxiety of not being wanted, loved or worthy. No matter how bad you feel, remember you belong in this life. You are worthy. Being wanted and loved naturally follow.

During the times we are not lonely and feel more centred, we are linked in to our life energy. We are part of life and do not suffer loneliness except perhaps fleetingly and are not bothered much by it. One way to relieve loneliness temporarily is to reconnect with the earth, to get outside and walk. Whether we go to the ocean or into a crowd at the shopping centre, these different experiences reconnect and put us back into relationship with life for a time.

Learning more about loneliness is helpful. Psychotherapist Robert Johnson says there are three types of loneliness. There is a kind of loneliness for the future, for what has not yet been realised and relationships we long for. There is loneliness for what is past; this aligns with grief. Then there is loneliness for god. I think of the third kind as a loneliness for beauty and nature.

Loneliness for the past, for our loved-one, overtakes us in grieving and it can spread to loneliness for the future and loneliness for god/beauty. We want to return to the happy times and places we had. Exaggeration of our happiness is normal, where we forget the tough and difficult times and glorify what made us happy—the comfort and security, or adventure and surprise—whatever quality characterised our relationship and life with the loved-one. It is a time of backward-looking.

Acceptance comes in our own good time. First we need time to remember, reflect and do the work of grief. Eventually we accept that we cannot re-enter the past world with our loved-one. However, when our backward-looking dominates life and thoughts and seems permanent, it becomes what is called regressive in psychological terms. This interferes with our ability to experience life now and find new enjoyment and fulfilment. Instead we continue to pine, all we want is for the other to return to our life again. This is what grief can morph into, but it is not the same as grief and mourning our loss. It is like a form of unrequited love. Loneliness for the past takes over becoming constant wishful thinking, and, because it cannot be fulfilled, it is spoils the life we have left to live. We become colonised internally by negative and ongoing pining. Yet our loss is irreversible. Continuing to pine and wish otherwise compounds loneliness and suffering.

We may believe we cannot bear the weight of the loss and will be crushed under its burden, but what is less painful and harrowing: accepting the loss, or living on and on, endlessly pining for what was?

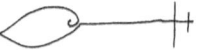

If you want to talk about being lonely, if you need to talk, first find the right person to talk to. Talking to someone ill-equipped to respond is a trap I have fallen into and sorely regretted. Beware talking to whoever is around or easily contacted. The person you always unload and chat to on the phone, the one you do yoga class with or the neighbour, may not be the one ready or able to give the listening and support needed. Pick those who can. Because we are vulnerable, an empty or ill-considered conversation can exacerbate isolation and loneliness. When someone you confide in has insufficient understanding or experience to deal with it, possibly misconstruing what the conversation is about, it can burn. If they miss seeing your vulnerability and instead see weakness and conclude you need someone to take control, that can diminish you. Your need for a compassionate friend may become all about them and their opinions even though they swear they are only looking after you. Instead, go to a competent friend, a mentor, professional counsellor or psychotherapist. Wait to talk to them if necessary. It is worth it.

Loneliness and Fear

There is fear associated with loneliness. Spending far too much unwanted time alone is a breeding ground for fears and exacerbates isolation. This is so for us all, and felt especially by our elderly living alone after the death of their life partner, leaving them vulnerable.

I want to make special mention of them with this heartwarming story. You may be elderly yourself or connected to someone elderly who is suffering a loss. Whatever your circumstances, this is a story about fear creeping into loneliness to make it worse.

"I feel so good... And look outside. It's raining. We need the rain."

These were the last words spoken by Kate before the light went out of her eyes. Her son, Peter, stood at her bedside, amazed and suddenly full of love. He had not heard her say she felt good for decades. Peter was moved to his core, they were his mother's last words.

Ten months earlier, Kate had moved into the nursing home. She had lived in their family home for sixty years and robustly resisted moving out after her husband died two years ago. His years with Alzheimer's were hard on her. She endured his long, slow deterioration and the final torment of him not knowing who she was.

After he died, Peter noticed she became thin and nervous. Kate refused to admit anything was wrong, but eventually he got Rosie, a counsellor he knew, to call in on her regularly.

Kate had become afraid to sleep. Over time, she opened up to her new counsellor friend, Rosie. When she slept, she had nightmares. She often heard strange noises at night too. That terrified her and she kept a hammer beside her bed.

The two talked about many things, including her husband's death. It wasn't long before Kate told Rosie that she had become afraid of dying since her husband died, and Kate realised she was to be next. It filled her with a fear that she had never known before. Rosie was concerned about her physical and mental suffering. Gently, Rosie introduced the idea of a nursing home where Kate would be safe and looked after. Kate recoiled. What about all her things? The furniture and crockery? What about the books and photos?

Between Peter and Rosie, they convinced Kate it was time to let go of the belongings so that she could be safe, secure and comfortable instead of isolated in a large house in need of repair. Reluctantly, and in desperation, Kate agreed.

Once settled in the home, Kate fell into the routine warily at first. Soon she found it a relief to have people around and not to have to shop and get her own meals. Every shopping trip had become a huge effort. It used to take her a long time to get dressed in the morning, especially in the cold, and walk to the nearby market for food. She came home exhausted.

Now her fears and the weight of her everyday burdens had lifted. The home was not perfect and there was one annoying old biddy, but Kate found it a huge improvement on the lonely life that she had been living. That last day when Peter came to visit she told him so, feeling safe and content.

"I feel so good... And look outside. It's raining. We need the rain."

Roots of Loneliness

Many times in life we crave peace and quiet with some space to catch our breath and have a rest from everyone and everything — from having to talk, socialise, lead, be there for others and still get done all the tasks of the day. The outward flow to the external world needs to stop for a time to allow us a chance to replenish ourselves and be in touch with our inner world. It doesn't mean we don't love or appreciate others. It recognises the need for the rejuvenation that time alone brings. Time to ourselves.

Some people voluntarily enter long periods of solitude for rest and restoration. It is regarded as having a spiritual or creative purpose. In comparison, loneliness is seen as an undesirable state that no one wants to own up to and everyone is scared of.

As young children, being left alone is frightening. Even though young children are resourceful when they have to be, in truth most of us wouldn't have got very far left on our own as a child for extended periods of time. We would be afraid without our parents to protect and look after us. Particularly because without their protection the world can quickly become a confusing and hostile place.

But as adults, although we can look after our selves, the frightening thoughts and emotions continue. Until we become aware of what is really going on, that is. The adult fear is not actual because if we are under threat now we will find ways to survive and be safe. We are no longer defenceless children. Whatever our circumstances, after the death of one we love, we can survive and live on with dignity. We take the necessary steps for our selves, because unlike a child, we can. The fear and anxiety that we feel so keenly is a left-over reaction from childhood when the fear of abandonment was truly terrifying. How would a small child survive and defend him or herself alone in the big world that was not yet understood?

That situation no longer exists. As adults the fear lingers, but is not real. We can look after our selves. There is no imminent danger to our life or safety.

As adults faced with loneliness, we can cease to fear being alone.

Know the Dark

Nights can be the worst in grieving and may feel like long, lonely ordeals. Nights do not have to be this way. We can befriend the night. Darkness has two aspects. One is fear of the unknown and what we cannot see, which stirs the dark imaginings that frightened us as children and now translate into adult fears. One way to think about these night fears is like dreams: they are of our own invention, the messages and symbols are from the soul about what we need to pay attention to within ourselves and our life. For instance, if there is a persistent fear of an intruder coming to rob us, we might ask what are we robbing our self of? How are we intruding on something we hold dear? What is taken from us that is needed for our wellbeing? When we get the right question, the rest will flow in terms of dismantling fears, one by one.

The night and the dark within blooms and sings with its own language and life. Night also brings the magical, romantic and mysterious. The magic will only die if we kill it off, otherwise we can revive it. The dark shelters us like a thick silent cloak we are wrapped into. The night is the time of love, of gazing at stars and wondering about the unknown and possibilities. Darkness brings us closer to our soul, wonderment, creativity, wellbeing. It releases our imagination, not to be afraid, but to be enchanted.

> The storm woke me with a fright through the night. I couldn't sleep yet again. I wrote, I read and thought. A lot. I thought about dying and meaning. Confronting my own death creates meaning for my life. Meaning is vital for a good life. It's what humans do to transcend suffering and light up life with insight, awe and hope.

Loneliness is feeling alone. We may truly be alone, or not really alone and perceiving it that way. We can be lonely in a group, when we are with friends or lonely in a marriage. Being alone is unavoidable. However, loneliness is associated with being dejected, rejected, isolated against our wishes and forsaken. All that breeds a state of mind that can exacerbate circumstances we find ourselves in, circumstances unwanted or unfamiliar or both, like bereavement, when time is spent alone and feeling lonely.

If negative thoughts take hold, then we start to see everything through that lens. A detrimental negative attitude compounds and we can get stuck in loneliness.

When feeling sad and downhearted, it can be easy for that to become a generalised negative outlook. We become negative about ourselves (for example, no one is interested in me; no one cares; I am unworthy); negative about others (not one person has given me a helping hand, they are all too interested in themselves); and negative about life (there are no jobs for me, I have no future, there's nothing to live for). What is critical is the meaning we attach to our experience and the way we interpret what is going on.

When Loneliness Becomes Self-pity

Loneliness invites self pity. Self pity is not the same as grief. Self pity moves into different territory where we feel sorry for our self that a dark time has overtaken us and there is little we can do to relieve it and be loved and loving again. This quickly builds the sense of being a victim.

Feeling like a victim means believing we are hopeless, powerless and defeated. That state of mind can be accompanied by resentment and other unhelpful emotions that restrict our capacity to think and act in ways to take care of living. The effect is to become passive and possibly manipulative in hoping for or actively seeking someone to rescue us.

Loneliness can be seen as a state of mind. Treating our self with kindness is an antidote. There are other antidotes which we'll get to. Remember that after losing a loved-one, whatever our relationship with them, we are wounded, possibly in trauma. We are vulnerable, which does not mean weak, it means opened out. We are more susceptible to dwell on emotions like loneliness and self pity. We can hold dear what is now past without defining our future in negative or defeatist ways. Rumi puts it so beautifully,

"The wound is the place where the Light enters you."

The etymology of the word lonely is helpful for thinking about loneliness. The original meaning of lonely from c.1600 was to "be lone, solitary"—you will note that "lone" is composed of "one". It was hundreds of years later that lonely became associated with the notion of being "dejected for want of company". In contrast, the etymology of the word alone is to "be all-one" and connected to oneness. This is a different idea, introducing the possibility of growth because being all-one is to be whole. All-one is a state of not being needy, of not pining for company because we are complete or sufficient on our own. It leads to a simple and empowering idea that has been around for hundreds of years. It is enjoying our own company.

There is a long-standing tradition of elders and the wise to retreat into periods of solo time for reflective contemplation. Leaders, writers and philosophers still do to this day to centre themselves, think and do inner work. This leads onto the notion of solitude.

When Loneliness Becomes Solitude

There is a difference between loneliness and solitude. Loneliness implies a situation forced upon us. There is no choice. With bereavement, that is the case. There is no choice about the loss. The sudden absence after the death of someone close leaves us feeling lonely for them. Disoriented. Shaken. For some people, their only source of intimacy is gone. Yearning for them can lead to neediness and grasping for something essential in life that is now missing. As time goes on, however, we recover our self.

With some conscious intention we can contrast loneliness with solitude. Solitude is spending time on our own. Solitude implies there is choice and purpose rather than a devastating or unfortunate situation forced onto us. I regard my solitude as a luxury. It is a practice of being sufficient within myself and the time of soulwork and discovery. A creative space for writing. I look forward to solitude and have become quite good at it, for many days and weeks on end (I admit, sometimes it gets too much). For the first half of life I got anxious with too much time alone, totally contradicting my fearlessness. It never occurred to me to ask why, until one year facing unavoidable loneliness, I enquired into what was going on. I hope it takes you far less time than it took me to unearth the underlying false belief, embedded way back in childhood.

Solitude is transformative, often entered into deliberately to explore and contemplate. Solitude is conducive to soulwork, healing and creativity. Whatever calming words may come from others, it is the time alone when much healing is done. That is when we find peace, courage and open out to new depths of meaning. Solitude is a beautiful place to be valued and protected. Through solitude, we come back home.

> "A human can be them self only so long as they are alone; . . . if they do not love solitude, they will not love freedom; for it is only when they are alone that they are really free. [Schopenhauer, "The World as Will and Idea," 1818] (Non-sexist language added)

Solitude is a time for growth and reconnecting with our soul. In solitude there is the freedom to return to the earth of our being, to take that descent into the ground of who we are and return rejuvenated.

A Change in Consciousness

Can you regard loneliness as a transition to something else? During the big transition passages like bereavement, while we are like pilgrims in unknown territory and sensitivities are more finely tuned, to spend time alone is to become receptive to what we need to learn.

We can find new friends and company which is pleasant and worthwhile, but we should be aware it treats the symptom not the cause. Resolution of loneliness is rarely found externally; it comes from within. When we stay with loneliness rather than try to fight or flee from it, a new consciousness arises. The change in consciousness turns loneliness into solitude. Or it happens the other way around, we turn loneliness into solitude which has the effect of transforming consciousness. Either way, we are in a different field of awareness this way with a different set of principles.

There are three qualities to mention for this change in consciousness: the fear of loneliness subsides, unconscious assumptions surface, and solitude becomes developmental.

The fear of loneliness subsides. We realise that being alone is not all that bad, even tough negative thoughts bubble up. In fact, being alone has certain advantages, in particular being able to please our self without imposing on someone else. We can do what we want, when we want, how we want. If we want to read until 3am, no problem. If we want to become vegetarian, we can do so without having to double shop or prepare separate meals. If we do an early morning walk every day, it is entirely up to us. Or if we have a long day working, or reading, or watching films, we go ahead without guilt or negotiation. We can reflect without interruption or concern.

We can enjoy our own company and please our self, possibly for the first time in life. This is the way it can be for you. It is legitimate to be happy alone and the world does not end. Solitude is the well-known, proven method to reach solace used by masters and ordinary folk the world over. Learning to like our own company and relax alone into the simple, everyday things of life are aspects of solitude.

Unconscious assumptions surface in the back of the mind. I mean false assumptions, fallacies that we've acted on ever since we can remember. For instance, the assumption that we need other people to be happy, to be safe, to be complete—need being the operative word. The realisation dawns that when we don't see those we know for some time, we are okay. It takes some getting used to, especially if the departed loved-one was in our life a lot. But we don't have to rush around trying to fill our time with other people or with someone who can take their place. We become more self-sufficient and don't have to rely on others for company. To expect they will provide a feeling of security and safety, or even a distraction from loneliness, is drawing a long bow anyway and rarely works. As a fully grown adult we can provide safety and security quite well for our self.

Solitude becomes developmental. This is the third and most profound aspect to a change in consciousness from loneliness to solitude. As we have discussed, solitude has a different quality to loneliness, a quality that beckons curiosity and gently relocates our centre of gravity. Solitude enhances psychological and spiritual growth in ways that cannot be done while we are with others. This is in itself starts to develop consciousness as perception and the way we think shifts to another level. When we add intent to the way we approach solitude, some wonderful experiences start to happen. All the spiritual teachings advocate periods of time alone in contemplation.

In short, solitude is not only a good time for personal reflection, but more a condition for developing consciousness, a big subject explored in my next book. The awareness of consciousness includes developing self-knowledge, ongoing self-examination, identifying and pursuing our life task and interpersonal capacities such as magnanimity, insight, courage and perfecting our love. This goes hand in hand with contemplation, and more on this can be found in Part IV, see Contemplation.

Solitude is Loneliness Evolved

There is some comfort in knowing that through many times and lives, others have had the experience of loneliness too. Loneliness is part of being human. Beyond that I found there is a purpose to my loneliness, captured by theologian and author on socio-spiritual themes, Thomas Merton, when he wrote, "Solitude is loneliness evolved to the next level of reality." We experience the same purpose. Those who transform loneliness into solitude gain peace of mind. Many become engaged in a sacred enquiry into consciousness. Paradoxically, solitude resolves loneliness.

From personal experience and counselling others, I have mapped a few general phases to progress loneliness from being debilitating and fearful to becoming solace and renewed consciousness.

Avoidance then Distraction

Initially, we make attempts to fight or flee from loneliness. Most often these attempts turn out to be unsatisfying, even empty.

Resignation then Confrontation

After avoidance, we resign and surrender to feeling alone. We confront loneliness, face its ordeal and fear its hardship. We can get stuck at the point of resignation to become cynical and bitter, unless we move on to the next phase.

Acceptance then Gratitude

Reaching acceptance: "Well, this is how it is. It is not so bad. It could be worse." Then taking time to be thankful for what we have rather than focus on what we lack and do not have, keeps self-pity at bay. Spend daily time on gratitude. See Part IV, Gratitude.

Realisation then Solace

After a time, we realise that loneliness is shifting to solitude. We start to appreciate solitude as valued time of solace for soulwork: reading, journalling, contemplation and ritual.

New Depth

Gradually, our solitude can become a spiritual time of discovery and enrichment.

Solitude as a path to deeper consciousness is a spiritual journey. Loneliness takes us through hell and back. To our amazement, we come out the other side of loneliness with new glimpses of heaven. It is not a substitute for the happiness we shared with our loved-one and have now lost, but there is a new sense that fulfilment and meaning are now possible. In the loving words of the great Irish poet, John O'Donohue:

> When you cease to fear your solitude, a new creativity awakens in you.
>
> Your forgotten or neglected wealth begins to reveal itself.
>
> You come home to yourself and learn to rest within.
>
> Thoughts are our inner senses.
>
> Infused with silence and solitude, they bring out the mystery
>
> of inner landscape.

Agents of Solace to Aid Loneliness

There isn't always someone available to give us comfort and support when it is most needed and we are left to our own resources. As mentioned already, the poets and spiritual teachers understand the depths of human experience and have been there before us. I love Buddhist philosophy for its ability to clean up the mind and shift thoughts to a bigger and wiser perspective. Following are some agents of solace to calm loneliness and facilitate a positive approach and shift of consciousness.

These experiences of nature, kindness, beauty, dreams and friends, become transformative as we calm our loneliness and enable our solitude.

Being in Nature as an Agent of Solace

Nature has powerful healing and restorative qualities. Here's what it can be like. Getting out into nature, especially where it is possible to be alone and quiet in our self, takes us outside the distractions of day to day life. Inside wilderness regions, parks and gardens we are outside all the social and physical structures that contain us everyday. It provides relief from the schedules, task lists, constant noise, traffic, computers, social media, expectations and commitments that build up in life. In nature we inwardly reflect the freedom and natural rhythms of the surroundings as we breathe fresh air and take in the sounds, sights and textures. As we go into nature more often, our observation and awareness sharpens and we appreciate the beauty and mysteries more. Our surroundings become a mirror to our soul.

Nature is a sanctuary for solitude. The Latin for nature is "solitudo". When we allow our selves to be immersed in nature we remember that we are part of the whole, a part of nature. Our spiritual belonging, an ease of being, a sense of wonder and inspiration is there to be discovered.

Kindness as an Agent of Solace

Adopting the intention of being kind to others takes us out of our own troubles and sorrow. Kindness is practical and generous. Remember to be kind to yourself as a way to look after yourself. As an example, when you're wide open and grieving, don't do things that exacerbate your pain and suffering.

Expect some changes in yourself as you grieve. For instance, if you are now prone to fear and easily spooked, don't do things that aggravate your fear, whatever that is, even things you used to enjoy like watching or reading thrillers. If you have a propensity to feel self-pity, then stay away from sad stories and documentaries of victimisation, and people you know who habitually talk like a victim. Equally, avoid rescuers in search of a victim to save, because you may find yourself slipped into the role of a victim for their rescue care. Seek the kindhearted instead. Grieving makes us more susceptible and sensitive. While you grieve, allow the reasoned, practical part of you to mind your life. Regard your rationality it as an agent of comfort.

Beauty as an Agent of Solace

Throughout grieving, seeing beauty can sustain us. The French philosopher Blaise Pascal wrote,

"In difficult times, carry something beautiful in your heart."

I've also heard this translated as, "Always keep something beautiful in your mind."

Whichever translation you prefer, the idea of holding something of beauty internally is healing. For example, I look for something new of beauty everyday. It's a little ritual to find something beautiful that I see in another person or in the surroundings to inspire the day. I set the intention in the morning and start the day with this in mind, hoping it will last a little longer every time.

We can learn to see beauty in unlikely places. When you look at an old coat or garment in your wardrobe, you can see it as an ordinary everyday thing. It is functional, nothing special. Or you can see that someone has woven the material and made the garment which involved a lot of work. Someone may have put much care and pride into the process. You can also see that old garment carries memories of your life that infuse it with meaning. So it becomes changed from being just an object in the background. When those memories of yours are loving, it becomes something of beauty in its own way. It is beautiful because of the memories you cherish.

Love as an Agent of Solace

In the spirit of seeing beauty, we need to be open to recognising how another expresses their love and does or says something beautiful. We all have an idea of what love and kindness is like to receive. It can be a spontaneous action that fills us with joy and gratitude, or something symbolic or a little celebration. A friend wanted her husband to bring her flowers every week to show his love was still alive. It carried much meaning for her because deep down she was afraid she was unlovable. Intuitively her husband knew this and, far from being a demanding chore, he lovingly brought flowers home.

If we think about it, we all have some set ideas on what actions show care for us. With those set ideas, we can miss actions we fail to see as loving. One example is tough love. When we are told something we do not want to hear, it's a bitter pill to swallow but in effect it frees us up or gives an invaluable insight. There are other examples, such as the person who avoids saying anything with words but says it through their actions. Like a friend who comes over unbidden to fix the broken washing machine, or do some chores that your loved-one always did, or lends you their dog for a whole long weekend because they are away one night. Then there are the people who say little, or say it clumsily, but when you pay attention you see there is love behind their actions. Listen carefully to hear the grace behind what others do and say. When you do this, when you recognise love and beauty, life is enriched a hundred fold and the giver becomes kindred.

Dreams as an Agent of Solace

It's worthwhile recording dreams on waking as they quickly slip away and out of mind. Not only the good dreams but the other ones that make an impact as well. The dream is something that we have created. It doesn't come from anywhere else but inside us. I look at every dream as a symbolic message from my unconscious, telling me what to pay attention to. Dream messages are cryptic and we need to pick up the clues and decipher the meaning; the message will make sense in our current context. So even bad or annoying dreams can have a gem of wisdom to show us and bear spending some time thinking about.

The following was a rare and beautiful dream that came to me in the middle of the lowest point in my grieving pilgrimage. I felt despairing and miserable.

The ambience was calm and balmy. My husband was with me, although in reality he had died many months before. In the dream he was close by and happily at his best. As I looked into the room from the open window behind us, I felt something brush past from behind my left shoulder. It touched my cheek. A large bird the size of a wild King Parrot had flown in and now glided around the room. The bird was many shades of blue with long exotic tail feathers. I was struck by its elegance in its slow flight. Soon it settled on my left within touching distance and stayed quite still and tranquil as I reached out.

Throughout the dream I felt serene. Contentment and peacefulness was mutual, in the air. After I woke it occurred to me that was the bluebird of happiness.

I awoke amazed and calmed, and wondered what on earth I was doing that I wasn't aware of, to keep the despair and mystery weighing so heavily on my shoulders, and prevent myself from accessing the beauty around me.

Friends and Circles as an Agent of Solace

After enough solo grieving time, there comes a time when we want some company again. It is up to us to reach out and indicate to others that now we are ready and want contact with them. You could call or write to ask how they are and that you would like to see them. We need not go far to make new friends, just need to be open to it. All we have to do is take the next step; stop to have a chat to a neighbour close by, someone in the local shop or library, or people who walk their dog in the same park. We start feeling lonely for what could be in the future, a future to be made by our own hands.

Community Groups as an Agent of Solace

One of the aspects missing from grieving is being held by a community. Generations ago, grieving was more of a community process, with opportunities to talk and hold ceremonies with neighbours and family. It can be a long, lonely process to go through the whole grieving journey alone. Circles and community groups set up for support and conversation about grieving bring grief out into the open. It is a relief to many to talk with others who are grieving. Sharing the way you feel and the experience you have been through can be comforting and liberating.

Chapter 8

Grieving as Sacred Process

To grieve is to meet the soul. It is a time to discern the difficult and uplifting truths of self, love and hope, and look into the shadows of our psyche. We sacrifice and let go what we love and at the same time, are confronted with what is lacking and no longer right with life that somehow must be addressed and put right. It is an ordeal of lament as we bleed from what we now lack.

As a sacred process, the ordeal of grief has meaning beyond a recovery. For some First Nations people, the word for lament means "to experience the voice of the sacred through sorrow". If we go with our lament, allowing it to take its course by neither minimising nor exaggerating it, we eventually come to the voice of the sacred through our longing. Rumi tells us the importance of this:

"It is the longing that does all the work."

Our longing changes the bitter to the sweet given time and attention. We see glimpses it is possible to be enchanted again with life. Our mind starts to follow our soul. We again see the rainbow and open our eyes to treasures in the world. We see life through the sheer silken threads of the sacred.

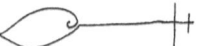

When there are no more barriers, your love can flow. Once the ending has come it is the culmination of your relationship. It is the conclusion of everything that it was and all it was not. Whatever experiences come with the ending, the ending itself has its own beauty when you are open to it. Even a painful death brings peace.

When I was deeply immersed in grief, after some time a feeling of oneness grew. I can only describe it as feeling beauty. Seeing beauty in the world—in raindrops and colour, in a vase that someone has lovingly crafted—was an experience of deep appreciation. It transformed the grief pilgrimage and the landscape of my mind.

Seeing and feeling beauty is part of experiencing grief as sacred.

Sacred process can be embraced and you can start to make it your own, a living presence within you. Sacredness, the embodiment of beauty, meaning and wonder, is transcendent.

Surrender

Surrender to grief. There is nothing to fight and fighting to suppress grief does not work. You can't fail at grief, only do it harder. Surrender, and let the grief process carry you as it has its own wisdom and sacred process. It is not something outside your self, the grief and sacredness is you. Trust your self. There is nothing to be afraid of. Grief is a direct link to your soul and inner beauty, an expression of love.

By the way, just in case you feel obliged, you do not have to force yourself to get out there and "keep living life". Having daily quiet time away from your usual interactions is good, and you may find it a welcome refuge, providing relief for private mourning. A walk in the park or a garden, feeling the wind on your face, sitting quietly at home—many of these things become sacred experiences in this heightened state, seen and felt anew as wonders of life.

Look for the little joys you now feel even without your loved-one beside you. These are times when sadness wells up, waiting to be expressed and set free. With some solitude and quiet, a spiritual essence comes to us, or comes from within us. We know without doubt when it is good for the soul.

Grieving and Feeling Unloved

Sometimes there can be grief over losing one who was not loved, or of losing a loved one who did not love us. People close to us do not always treat us well and may even have been abusive. Abuse can take many forms: withholding love and affection, manipulation, psychological abuse including systematically destroying self-worth, domination, threat, sexual abuse and financial abuse. It is not an exhaustive list. Grief opens up these wounds.

Some people endure terrible entrapment for years. For others their abusers are not central to life any longer, but on the periphery such as an ageing parent. As adults, we put up with abuse because there seems to be no choice, or we are bound by loyalty, vows, religious decree or social dictum. There may be a threat of not being believed by family or community and having to justify ourselves or be left alone if we withdraw from the abuser. Dealing with our own conscience if we abandon them can cause complications and even hardship.

Sometimes, after their death, you can realise your love for this person, despite fearing them for their abusiveness, avoiding them, hating them, or being angered to distraction by them. With a bitter and manipulative aged parent, for instance, after their death you might better understand what role their past life played in causing their actions or in adding to their attitude. You may see that their actions were unconscious, an ineffective way of trying to get fragile hidden needs met. There is much literature available on trauma and the motivation of abuse.

Saddest of all, you may understand that with their abuse, they loved you the only way they could because they were damaged and abused themselves and had never healed.

We mourn for all that could have been. The depth of that grief can be astonishing. It goes back to our ancestors. What once caused anger now brings sadness as we face the sum of what they denied themselves but forced onto us, thinking they were doing the best thing, or the only thing. There is no longer hope of any reprieve.

It is with great sorrow we say goodbye when we felt unloved. But in so doing, we free ourselves and deepen our hearts. I hope this little section has led you to reconsider whether you really were unloved, or the next link in an unconscious chain of suffering and trauma passed on from one generation to the next.

Quest

If you have once had the privilege
of caring for another
who is trampled, frail or angry
even though you are wounded
and battered by life
or lost, harrowed, wretched
yet still you generated care, then
you know what it is to live with soul

Without soul the forest breath seems dead
birdsong canopies bring no delight
and life bears no fruit.
We are haunted by memories
of what we hoped and now lack

But descend into the valleys
and caves of consciousness
back to the underground river
with its shared waters of truth
there drinking slowly
get ready to do your Task

So that an age after we are dead
children will have forests
sunrise and stars
while elders make their descent
to reclaim the river
of wisdom, beauty and grace.

Journal Note: A Sacred Reflection

Being taken back while going forward. The memory of spending the last six months with you flooding into me now it is all over. Knowing again the song of your soul like a clear note that rang through all the past words, harsh thoughts, that confronting high bar you set for your life. Things you said sometimes landing well; sometimes crashing with astonishing insensitivity until, in the end, there you lay. Silent. Your eyes unseeing. Your heart tired and at rest. Your body empty.

As I walked away, leaving the sight and feel of you forever, I filled with anguish and love for an all too-human life, for a man who believed with all his mind that he must be more than he was. Who met his own disappointment with courage and retracted harsh judgements because in the end, there was no one there to judge. Instead, what emerged was the young soul from long ago, the soul of the pure-hearted boy that your older sister knew so well. Two little children in war-time Holland, faithfully looking after the younger ones. The stories stung my heart.

You said you lived a selfish life, and later how grateful you were for our love. Love was your anchor on the precipice of free-fall into the abyss. The abyss awaited you, and you inched toward it without a fight. I faced an abyss too as my life stretched on alone. Together we took courage as we went our separate ways.

Doing Something for your Loved-One

Consider doing something for the one who has died, something to honour them. It could be something they started but didn't finish, or something in your own life that would make them proud. It might be something for yourself, to aid healing and digest all that has happened. There could be a project, something to pass on, conclude or build on their behalf, or some volunteering work to continue or start up.

I decided to continue our mentoring work but make writing my central contribution. Also to go on a pilgrimage. I wanted to walk alone in nature, somewhere that was safe enough, beautiful, and that would stretch me physically and mentally. Martin and I spend a lot of time together, in the wilderness fishing and camping, and on our farm where we planted several thousand trees. All that was now past. So I started my search for the right pilgrimage: the Camino de Santiago looked good — 500 miles from France through the Pyrenees to the west of Spain. The other consideration was the demanding Kumano Kodo in the southern mountains of Japan's Kii Peninsula. That was the one I favoured.

In the end, I did neither. Instead, I gave a more direct contribution to others by presenting at an international conference in Italy called Science and Nonduality. That is where this book was born as others asked to know more about "standing in the fire". My talk was called 'Beautiful Endings' with more emphasis on grief as an opening to consciousness development. It included more Buddhist teachings and philosophical applications, including David Bohm's theory of the implicate and explicate order. I had never been to Italy and had only a few basic Italian words (mainly about food), so travelling alone I was well out of my comfort zone. But it worked out well. I saw some of the most beautiful countryside and small ancient townships I'd ever seen on route to the conference in the ancient Castle of Titignano with my dear friends, Geoff and Georgina, who gave moral and technical support for my presentation. Thankfully, the treacherous mountain roads were navigated by ex-racing car driver, Geoff. At the week-long conference I met new friends from all over the world. Although it was wonderful being in a strange land, I felt terribly lonely. It was just over a year after Martin died.

Out of that pilgrimage, for myself as well as for loved-ones dead and gone, this book was born together with my resolve to be a full-time writer.

Chapter 9

Mystics and Spiritual Teachers

Grief is private and an individual process with differences for us all. What we share is to find some meaning in grief because that contributes to reaching peace of mind. Finding meaning is also an early sign of recovery, that we are moving from the initial aching stage of feeling we are burning in the fires of grief. Before us, many philosophers, poets and people in everyday life have experienced the grief and aloneness of losing someone loved and irreplaceable. Here is what five spiritual teachers say about living and dying. They share a universal acceptance of the cycle of life and death with differing philosophies about consciousness. Their words represented here are just a taste of what has been their life's work, I hope enough to fire up a strength that lies within you, and an energy that flows. Their enquiry, thoughts and sense of mystery are timeless, and even though some of these words are centuries old, they still soothe and have relevance today. It is spiritual. It is sacred.

Theology

Meister Eckhart was a thirteenth century German theologian, mystic and philosopher. After coming to prominence with a large following, in later life he was accused of heresy, a political tactic, and brought before an Inquisition. Eckhart died before a verdict was received. Today he has status as a great mystic from philosophical scholars and within contemporary popular spirituality.

Meister Eckhart's most relevant work of death and dying is titled, the Book of Divine Consolation. It contains practical advice to the grieving widow, the Queen of Hungary, who lost her mother and, three months later, her husband and children. Eckhart's essential advice is gold if you will take it on. He advises this:

When you suffer loss, you do not need compassion.

You need a different mindset.

Eckhart explains that you should think in a different way about loss, in this case advising Queen Angela's devastating loss of her husband and close family. It meant losing political and financial security as well. Eckhart's basic message is to detach. The reason he puts forwards as to why detach, needs close attention and some deep consideration.

Loss as a Delusion

It is human to fear loss and become anxious about the consequences. Nearly everyone experiences the fear of losing someone and worries about what effect it will have on life and wellbeing. However, Eckhart goes on to point out the way this mindset is detrimental and does no good. His counsel is that loss is a logical consequence of delusion. It is the delusion of possession. People live with loss and suffer loss because they live with an illusion of owning something, of owning someone. In the case of the Queen it was the illusion of owning her husband, children and the kingdom. But Queen Angela did not own anyone. No one owns anyone else, nor any status or entitlement of office.

Everything is temporary. Everything passes in and out of life. Our own body is included, just as this day and this moment is included.

You suffer because of transitory things. You can not hold onto them. They are not yours. Let them go in your mind and be grateful.

Finally, Eckhart advises to be free of consolation. Do not expect, look for, or believe there is consolation to be found from any living creatures. You will not find it there. Consolation comes only from inside you.

Death as Going Home

John O'Donohue was a theologian, priest, philosopher and poet. In contrast to Meister Eckhart, he had many more warmhearted things to say about death and dying, with a gentler approach. I'll capture just a few of them here. He believed we can transform the fear of death, in so doing we free ourselves so that we fear little else. He spent much time in solitude after he left the priesthood, walking his beloved Celtic landscape and incorporating the Celtic spirituality and wisdom into the philosophies of Hegel in particular and his religion.

John O'Donohue taught that when the soul leaves the body, it is free of space and time; distance and separation are no longer containers to restrain us. The dead are our closest neighbours and are all around us. They do not travel to some far distant place where we cannot contact them. The eternal world is not another place. It is a different state of being. Much of John O'Donohue's teachings serve to soothe and calm, introducing people to new ways of being: "When you acknowledge the integrity of your solitude, and settle into its mystery, your relationships with others take on a new warmth, adventure and wonder."

Here are more of John O'Donohue's heart-warming words to you, an excerpt from his beautiful poem, A Blessing for Death:

May you know in your soul

that there is no need to be afraid.

When your time comes, may you be given

every blessing and shelter that you need.

May there be a beautiful welcome for you

in the home that you are going to.

Buddhism

The great Tibetan Buddhist lamas say that for up to twenty-one days after a person dies they are more connected to the previous life than to the next life. So for this period in particular, according to Sogyal Rinpoche, the loved-ones of the dead can be encouraged to continue their private communication with the deceased person and to say their goodbyes, wrap up any unfinished business, reassure the dead person, encourage them to let go of their old life and to move on to the next. It is reassuring even just to talk to the dead person and at some level to know that they are probably receiving your message. The mind of the deceased person at this stage can still be subtle and receptive.

Buddhism has much to say about dying and living well. In particular, the Buddhist philosophies on impermanence, attachment and suffering are helpful for grieving and coming to terms with death. I love Buddhism for its capacity to clean up the mind and set thoughts straight.

Part of the Buddhist approach to dying is karma and rebirth or reincarnation. The term karma is often misused in everyday language to mean "your just deserts" usually as a punishment, but in the Buddhist tradition karma means much more. Karma refers to actions taken, driven by intention, good and bad, which lead to consequences. My understanding is what we learn and apply from the consequences of our actions is the point of karma, and each successive life brings opportunities for further growth. Karma is carried forward in time from one lifetime to the next. In this way we learn to progress our consciousness and refine our intention to reflect compassion and mindfulness. The cycle ceases after many reincarnations when we have perfected consciousness.

The stream of consciousness moves from one life to the next. Consciousness as it is used here is not the same as cognition, nor does it include memory. It is more like the soul or spirit that continues, always knows itself, and informs our living once we learn to listen.

Impermanence

The Buddha's final words were about impermanence. There are various translations but all with the same theme: "Impermanence is inescapable. Everything passes away and vanishes. Therefore there is nothing more important than continuing the path with diligence."

The death of someone close is inescapably painful. No one can get away from it and we all feel pain and suffering. It is even more difficult for those emotionally and psychologically dependent on that person. We can be fooled into thinking relationships are forever, which may be what we promise each other in a love relationship or a close friendship. Deep down we all know the truth. There will one day be a separation. Nothing that exists is permanent. Everything is transitory. It is the inescapable fact of life that sooner or later we must realise. Impermanence is the central existential predicament we each face as humans.

Everyone knows this at some level. The car or computer won't last forever, and old Gran who has become estranged in the nursing home will die one day. The high from winning a game or being recognised for our contribution is only temporary and does not last, so we look to the next goal and the next high. It is only when someone close dies that we understand impermanence at a deeper level.

Attachment and Suffering

The path just referred to above is the path to enlightenment. This path is also the path to the cessation of suffering. Buddha claimed his teachings were essentially about suffering, its origin, cessation and path. The attachment to positive, negative and neutral sensations and thoughts is the cause of suffering, especially:

Greed and desire

Ignorance or delusion

Hatred and destructive urges

It is the attachment and the actual negative thoughts and powerful emotions that give rise to suffering. Buddhism teaches to recognise these negative states when they arise and assist them to pass. This is the opposite of what usually happens, that we cling to the negative thinking and emotion as the "source" of the problem. We identify the cause of suffering outside ourselves and the cause is blamed, condemned, punished or feared. Mostly, that cannot happen when someone dies. Then we are thrown back to concentrating on the reality and pain of loss and eventually on healing.

In Buddhism, death is not regarded as a final extinction. It is a waiting area until a further life is found, a new body to inhabit for another lifetime. Buddhists call this waiting space Bardo, the time after death and before our next birth. Consciousness continues in Bardo but without a physical body.

Fear of Death

The clear message from Buddhism is that death is not something to be feared, because fearing death distorts the ability to live well. Chinese philosopher, Chuang Tzu, was addressing suffering and the fear of death as long ago as the fourth century BC:

> The birth of a human is the birth of their sorrow. The longer they live, the more stupid they become, because anxiety to avoid death becomes more and more acute . . . The thirst for survival makes them incapable of living in the present. (Non-gender language added.) Cited by Sogyal Rinpoche.

Contemplation of death is regarded as an important practice. This is because (1) we realise how short and treasured life is and so do our best to make it meaningful and (2) By being familiar with the process of death and dying we will not be afraid when we die and will have a good death, which affects a good rebirth. The contemplation focusses initially on three roots:

Death is certain

The time of death is uncertain

What will help at the point of death is our inner development.

Each of these roots has implications that points the way to living well.

Nonduality

Rupert Spira is an international teacher of the New Science of Consciousness and direct path method of spiritual self-enquiry through his talks and writing. He is also a notable English potter with work in public and private collections. Spira is a frequent teacher at the international Science and Nonduality (SAND) conference.

In spirituality, nonduality means not-two, undivided, whole. Nondualism primarily refers to a mature state of consciousness in which the dichotomy of I/other is transcended. Nondualism is derived from one of the most ancient and enduring spiritual teachings, Advaita Vendata. Descriptions of nondual consciousness are found in most major religions including Christianity, Buddhism, and Hinduism. The words following are complied from the live presentations of Rupert Spira and, to the best of my ability, represented according to his meaning.

The fear of death—the fear of ceasing to be, to feel, sense, think, to have ideas, have an identity—all these fears will disappear. This happens every day when we sleep. In deep sleep, there is no body, no history or future, no worries from the past. All disappear in deep sleep. Further, it is a state we look forward to.

Our identity overlaps with our thoughts, feelings, sensations, each runs into the other. We believe they are us. That is not the case, we have them. Yet we invest our whole identity in them. Thoughts, feelings and sensations are not who we are. They are not the Self.

The remedy is to know yourself as you truly are. Go to the experience of your awareness. Of pure awareness. The experience is you. The experience of being. It is always constant. But we become detached from the Self when we get mixed up with thoughts and feelings and don't distinguish between them and our awareness, our being.

Ask yourself, what do I refer to when I say "I"? What is the I aware of? For instance, I am aware of the room. I am aware of my feelings. I am aware of my thoughts. Try emphasising "I am aware . . ." Regardless of what you are aware of, you have the capacity of awareness, of consciousness. That experience is peace itself. It gradually purifies itself. The fear and the loss will wither away due to neglect — it is no longer being fed by your interest.

This is not an intellectual process. It is one of loving awareness. I am not only aware. I am eternally aware. I am not a witness in the background. I am intimately one with all experience. It forms as a kind of conviction.

Consciousness

Consciousness is infinite. The body is finite. In a dream there is no body, we become infinite. Consciousness knows its own being and has no need to take the form of the finite mind. If consciousness wants to know the world it has to narrow, to zone in, to see the world from the body-mind. When the body dies, one particular aspect of consciousness disappears. The body-mind is a localisation of consciousness. The mind is like a whirlpool in a stream. When the body dies, the whirlpool disperses, but the water is still there. The whirlpool is like a finite mind. The body exists in the mind. Leaving behind the body happens when we sleep. Or when we have a new perception and then it passes.

All there is to the mind is thoughts and images. Awareness is independent of the mind and part of consciousness. When the mind disappears, awareness continues. We fear death because we have confused our identity with our body-mind.

Yet consciousness does not need the body-mind. We have always known this. In death, as in sleep, consciousness continues. There is nothing to fear as Rupert Spira puts it elegantly:

> Everyone is in search for something ...
>
> the scientist calls it Understanding
>
> the artist calls it Beauty
>
> the lover calls it Union
>
> and others call it Happiness.

The following are thoughts on death from author and teacher, Jeff Foster. He studied Astrophysics at Cambridge University, then embarked on a spiritual quest for the ultimate truth of existence. The spiritual search came crashing down with the clear recognition of the non-dual nature of everything, and the discovery of the extraordinary in the ordinary. He writes:

"Death? Where is death right now? Surely right now, all you can find is aliveness, life, the present appearance of everything right here and right now. Where is death? Death is always a projection, a story about something that will 'happen' in the future. But that story only ever happens right now."

Foster goes on to describe the Buddhist teaching of a wave, moving through the ocean. It approaches the shore (its apparent destination) and crashes onto it. The wave doesn't appear to be there any more. But has the wave gone anywhere? The wave has not disappeared; there was never a separate wave to begin with. It was never born as a separate identity so it cannot disappear. There was only the ocean, appearing temporarily as a wave. The wave went nowhere. There was no destination except the absence of the one wave that would reach the destination. A non-existent wave cannot die.

It is the same with death. In life we think we are the wave. In truth we are part of the whole ocean.

Sufism

Rumi was a thirteenth century Persian poet, Sufi mystic, Islamic scholar, philosopher and lover of humanity. His great masterpiece, the Mathnavi-I Ma'navi, translated, 'The Treatise Devoted to the Intrinsic Meaning of All Things'. This work is regarded as his magnum opus, and was dictated in its entirety to his faithful student over the course of twelve years. Rumi's influence today transcends national borders and ethnic divisions. He has been described as the best-selling poet in the United States, Europe and elsewhere around the world. Rumi's poetry has been translated into many languages, including English, German, Turkish, Arabic, French, Italian, Russian, and Spanish, and is being presented in a growing number of formats, including musical concerts, workshops, readings, dance performances and other artistic creations. Rumi's poems are heard in churches, synagogues, Zen monasteries and community gatherings.

Rumi's compelling and positive words are evocative, mysterious and universal. On death he says:

This place is a dream. Only a sleeper considers it real.

Then death comes like dawn, and you wake up laughing

at what you thought was your grief.

Known as the most widely read poet in the West, Rumi's thoughts, poems and teachings are widely acknowledged, regardless of caste, creed and religion. UNESCO celebrated 2007 as the Year of Rumi. Centuries after his death, his words not only inspire but also restore. His words on death are comparatively few, but just as potent as his word on love and esteem. He was well acquainted with death and grieving.

When Rumi was thirty-seven, he met the spiritual holy man, Shams, who changed his life. Prior to this meeting, Rumi had been an eminent professor of religion and a highly attained mystic. After their friendship he became a visionary poet and lover of humanity. Shams' companionship with Rumi was inspired but brief. Shams suddenly disappeared, not once but twice, leaving Rumi bereft and grieving. With the first disappearance, Rumi's son searched for him and found him in Damascus. The second time proved to be final, and local information was he had been murdered by Konyan citizens who resented Shams' influence over Rumi. In grief for Shams' death, Rumi's thoughts went to love and compassion for others confronting death:

... you must never think I am missing this world.

Don't shed any tears, don't lament or feel sorry.

... don't cry for my leaving.

I'm not leaving;

I'm arriving at eternal love.

In Sufism, death is seen as a way of attaining high spiritual life. In a good life, the liberation from ignorance is sought. In death, after a life well-lived over many reincarnations, the attainment of truth the ultimate reality is reached. It is a specialised and divine knowledge. The remembrance and contemplation of death during life is seen as a path toward knowledge. Striving to be free from earthly traps, such as the pleasures of the world, is an important remembrance. It emphasises the trap of ego and the worth of unselfish love. A Sufi prophet often quoted said, "People are asleep and when they die, they awake."

Psychotherapy

I include psychotherapy briefly, as most of the offerings are focussed on the fear and dread of death or stages of grief, rather than a philosophy of death and dying. In particular, existential psychotherapist, Irvin Yalom, has much to say from the point of view of the fear of death and engages readers with his writing and discernment. Carl Gustav Jung recognised that death is inevitable for everything living and to deny death is to deny instinct. In terms of attitude toward death, he said one should live as though we have centuries ahead and keep looking forward to the day in front, even though we know we are all going to die.

The main writer I want to mention here is Viktor Frankl. His philosophy, born of his devastating war experience and confrontation with death and suffering, is that as humans our lives must have meaning if we are to survive. After he survived the concentration camp of Auschwitz himself, he later found his wife and mother died there in the most brutal circumstances. In a letter at that time he wrote, "I am terribly tired, terribly sad, terribly lonely. I have nothing more to hope for and nothing more to fear. I have no pleasure in life, only duties, and I live out of conscience."

During this indescribable time of grief and anguish he writes his great work, 'Man's Search for Meaning' for publication and for his own recovery. His letter goes on, "No success can make me happy, everything is weightless, void, vain in my eyes, I feel distant from everything. It all says nothing to me, means nothing. The best have not returned (also, my best friend was beheaded) and they have left me alone."

As his life goes on, however, he begins to recover with a remarkable resilience. Frankl starts to see life again in a larger dimension. He writes that he increasingly sees life as meaningful, that in suffering and even failure, there must still be meaning, and we must find the meaning. That is what makes the human spirit magnificent and gives us the will to go on, even in the most dire of circumstances.

Frankl's life is an unforgettable story of transcendence from the horrors of mass murder and the death camps. He made the most of his psychologically and spiritually crippling experiences, to rise above them and transform them to a gift of great meaning and significance for the world.

Chapter 10

A Pilgrim's Journal Extracts

During the initial grieving process, people trying to give help by being positive were of no comfort. I wanted to give voice to the grief and loss that was the centre of my world, yet had no confidence that others were able to hear it. It was a lonely time. It seemed to be what I needed. I had no interest or inclination to see a grief counsellor and preferred to rely on my intuition and inner resources. With that, I could at least delve down to the depth of feeling and exploration needed. It is different for everyone.

Besides missing the companion I knew so well, the simple things, like sharing the little stories of the day, became what I longed for. As time went on I decided my north star was also what I longed for. The longing was the catalyst that showed what I needed to feel more alive. Now as I write this two years after his death, my task is to find new ways to fill these longings.

The following extracts are compiled from some daily journal entires during the first year after my husband died. I assure you my experience was immensely sorrowful but not morbid, and became what I can only call sacred. Here is my distilled grief journey, written over the first twelve months after his death, put together from daily journal entries. I don't know if your journey is anything like this, but I offer these extracts to bring you some companionship as a fellow pilgrim.

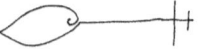

A Week After He Died

While he was dying our love became pure. It was unconditional goodness. There were times over the years it had not been like this. Nothing like this. It was some years back I had left him, only to return later as both of us suffered so much being separated. He was a strange man. As he aged he had become impossible and cranky. Then the two years he was so sick were different and his harsh edge lessened. In the last few months it vanished and our relationship became more than it had been before. It filled me with love.

My intuition and heart said he was dying. My mind wanted evidence, certainty, but that was not to be until the last ten days when the doctors said there was nothing more they could do. Heart and mind held on to hope until the last few weeks. He had been in and out of hospital for over eighteen months, and frequently since the massive operation last year. I spent every day in hospital with him, this last time for a month. Seeing him distressed was the hardest part. I go over and over the time leading to his death. Could I have done anything that would have made a difference, if not to the outcome because his body gave way, then to being with him? I suspect everyone goes through this awful self-assessment. I talk to myself as though he is here.

Two Weeks After He Died

It is now two weeks since my sweetheart died. I was with him when he died. Each in our own way, we yielded to forces far greater than ourselves. He departed. I stayed alone. It will be the funeral in a few days. We delayed it to wait for Yvette, his daughter and my step daughter who I love, to arrive back from overseas. Two weeks feels like an eternity.

My grief wracks me to the core. The pain is crushing. I am so grateful for my life, for the precious family and friends I love and who love me. Keeping that in mind seems to help a little. And yet I yearn for some relief. Just one day, one moment without the pain. Just some time where my heart does not feel heavy. A day I can wake without crying. A morning that I can see the sunrise and feel the freshness of the air without heartache. Without being overcome.

It is as though the sense of who I am is disappearing. For sure, the life I know has gone. What is there for me to hang onto? It feels like there is nothing there.

It is autumn. In the middle of my despair the leaves on the trees are stunning in their colours. They fall to the ground and look magnificent. I'm awe struck.

I have focussed everything on the funeral for what seems ages. There are so many arrangements. Really, I have just taken over the whole thing, but the family seem happy for me to do that. I'm grateful. I don't think anyone else wants the job or knows what to do. I'm clear on what Martin wants, his favourite music and he told me how he wants everything to go. Hopefully I've looked after family and considered friends and not neglected anyone. Now it is nearly here. I feel a lot of dread. And relief. Both at once.

An idea struck me. Because I have to sell our farm now and live in the city, I have to keep nature in my life. I know what I could do. Run mini pilgrimages for people, something that we can do in one day. I'll call it Little Pilgrimages. For later. I feel some hope.

It's a big transformation from Martin so fully in my life to no presence there at all. Nothing. Seems unbearable, impossible at times. I'm getting on with my writing, and dealing with the urge to buy men's farm shirts and socks on special before realising, yet again, that Martin is not here! How is it possible that a human is here walking around and talking, then suddenly they are completely gone? Vanished.

Time stretches out. Not in the sense that it drags or goes slowly. It is in the sense that yesterday seems like it was days ago. I think about a text message I want to reply to and when I look at it I'm astounded to see it arrived only yesterday, not last week as I thought it had. The funeral was just five days ago now, yet it seems more like five weeks. My perception of time is being stretched out and the fabric of time is spun differently.

Six Weeks After

It's now six whole weeks since he died. I have no longer been looking for what I can hang on to. Instead, the opposite—I've been letting go. Allowing the grief and pain to be there. Trusting my pain. When I started doing this a deep spiritual journey became central. It's become vital and constant. Somehow, the spiritual and mystery is keeping me company. I hope this isn't too crazy, but I don't really care two hoots about that, just a passing thought. The pain has not gone away, but I'm no longer afraid of it. I no longer wish the pain was not there with me.

Now it is winter. It's freezing, but I don't care and go out into the garden often. The European trees are bare, their branches fragile against the sky. It fills me with sadness as I remember his strong limbs that became so thin and fragile. I move on. Looking closely at the branches on my favourite Canadian maple against the bleak sky. This is the shade tree we would gather the family under in summer. Memories fill me with gladness and sad wistfulness.

There are times that I doubt my sanity. It adds to the feeling of descending into a well of despair. These are the times I'm at my lowest, when gloom and hopelessness overtake and there is nothing positive in the long months stretching ahead. When I realise I'm becoming depressed, I try to take myself in hand. I tell myself, "Remember this for the future! This will work. Go out into nature, walk in a forest or on the beach. Or go out among people; go to a big shopping centre or to the local market. Write this down and stick it on the wall so you don't get amnesia about it." Strangely, it brings some relief.

Overall, the grief itself has taken me deeply inside myself in a way that I see things with fresh eyes. Here I've found a sad but beautiful state. An awareness of all the beauty in the world. I write about it every day. I've been writing poetry in the garden in the cold. I wrote a poem called 'Beautiful Endings'. First draft.

Three Months After

Well, now I've started to observe myself, to be the detached witness to my grieving. I'd forgotten all about it until now, been too caught up with feeling devastated. Just noticing now. Not putting any value onto it, completely judgement free, but seeing what interpretations and meanings spring up that I attach to my thoughts, feelings, events. Some are mad when I step back and look at them. So I rein those in.

The witness part of me calms and counsels. As I write this I see there is a commentator part looking at the observer part! I'm aware of my awareness and doing a running commentary. The witness can see grieving doesn't mean I'll never recover, that I will feel all this pain forever. I know deep down that grief will lessen over time. I've experienced it before. How many times now? The grief will not go on forever and ever. It is simply that right now I am crying. Mourning. It is all right. Then the intensity will subside. I'll be all right.

The witness, the observer in me comes from a higher place. A higher consciousness. It's not new but feels so needed right now. I encourage the witness. Encourage is a fitting word and the witness brings me courage and perspective. When I feel emptiness, despair, the witness is like a benevolent companion with feet on the ground. It pulls me back from going down the dark well of despair and staying stuck there. The trip down the well is pivotal—painful but always a deepening of the spiritual experience. It's full of sorrow, but also enriching. Strange. The problem has been getting stuck at the bottom, lingering far too long in a cold and woeful underworld. My witness sees that I am okay, registers if I need anything and has the presence of mind to organise it, outline the steps I must take. Especially the ascent back from the depths of the well.

But the real saviour, the gold that has been uncovered and shines so brightly in my little world, is the spirituality of grief. It is sacred. It has opened something deeper within, immersed me in wonderment and mystery. In seeing beauty.

Now I want to be alone and look forward to returning to this state. I want to be in nature, on my own in the garden with the birds, to see the sunrise and the sunset. Then I feel blessed. Sometimes I imagine he is present in the twilight sky. He is released. Gone somewhere unknowable while I am here. I have a life to live, with or without grief. I plan the first Little Pilgrimage.

Six Months After

It is November. Mid spring. The long cold, dark of winter has finally receded. Sunshine, spring flowers, new bright green leaves on the trees and longer days help life seem less gloomy. It has taken months of work to get the farm ready for sale. Sadly and thankfully it was auctioned last month. I must move out in February. Now comes the onerous task of clearing out the house, the six sheds all nearly as big as the house, and all the machinery.

All his things are still here. It hasn't felt right to take them away. I got rid of his everyday things, like his crossword puzzles and things he always kept close by in the sunroom. What always upset me most is seeing his reading glasses, just there where he left them, waiting on the table beside his chair. I could not move them for months. Now I've put them in his drawer. But soon I must dispose of all these things. His tools and machines, his shoes, raincoat, all his suits, medicines—everything. The family will help and take what they want. I spend another sad sunset outside and go to bed as soon as it's dark.

For a few months now I've been turning over the idea that next year I must have something positive to look forward to. This is the witness again, looking out for me. If the long year stretches out ahead with nothing to lift it, I will get depressed and lonely. I have decided to do a pilgrimage. An inner and outer journey that is both physically demanding and spiritually uplifting. The Santiago de Camino from France to Spain looked good initially. On further investigation, the time of year when the weather is best is the time the trail is crowded. I need solo time. Time to recalibrate life. I started searching in Japan and elsewhere.

The warmer weather brings snakes out of hibernation. We have always had snakes at the farm, but never close to the house like this. Yesterday I nearly stepped on a medium size tiger snake that darted across the path in front of me, headed under the house. Over one and a half meters long, as round as my lower arm. See one and there are half a dozen you don't see. Am I nervous? You bet. Tiger snakes are aggressive and their venom is lethal. I've seen tigers and red bellied blacks twice the size elsewhere on the property and not been spooked. Now I've lost my nerve. Recently the neighbours have found half a dozen smaller ones and killed them. Where are the snake parents? I've started to confine myself to around the house and garden and even that doesn't seem safe any more. I'm constantly on the look out for snakes on the ground and in the trees and because of the threat, will be glad to leave here. There will be more of them in summer. The worry is if one gets inside the house as they're prone to do.

Back in Melbourne I've been running some Elders Circles for people transitioning from midlife. It's hard to keep promoting it and a great friend, Geoff, has been an enormous help and is very enthusiastic about all this. I wonder if I'm still too involved in grief to do it well. Somehow, though, the grief seems to help. More than ever, I want to connect soul to soul, and feel this is what we all miss now in life and seek vicariously. I lead the way and steer talk away from the weather for too long. I offer thoughts on living and dying, then too late, realise it is too much.

Twelve Months After

It is autumn again. A whole year has gone by. I no longer have the farm. I don't live in the country any more. My life has contracted literally and metaphorically from open spaces to my apartment. The first Christmas without him was very sad and strange. I'm blessed to have such a loving family and spent time with my daughter, son-in-law and grandchildren. My adult stepchildren came for Christmas Day too with their kids. It was strange and sad and lonely not having the big lunch at the farm for the family. There were no big preparations for me to do. Just helping. But that's how it is now, and I have to get used to it. Kim, my daughter, has taken my place as the head of family dinners.

Time is something I value more than ever before with a renewed appreciation that my time is finite. There is no need to fill up the spaces in the day, and although there are plenty of spaces, they are fertile voids where anything can happen that needs to happen, reading, imagining, cleaning, a poem, cooking, music, walking along the river. Writing is central every day, and I've extended my writing schedule to the whole morning at least from 6am to 11am. I don't accept work because I need the money if it's not what I want to do. So far so good and financially I'm doing well on less. I realise with surprise, I no longer go out at night. I go to bed early and raise early. Hardest of all, I say no when invited to anything my gut says is not right for me right at present. That has included dinner with friends and events that would have been good for networking. Getting clear means doing an inner search to bring out what agenda I'm following as distinct from what is actually good for me and what I love. It's trusting my innate wisdom. This feels good.

I treasure my time alone and sure have plenty of it. Sometimes far too much and I go for several weeks seeing no one I know in person. I'm lonely at times, but not ready to meet new friends and quite happy writing in my solitude. A few dear, close friends work with me on some projects for which I'm grateful and feel happy. I enjoy their company and the context of the work. (Amazingly, the first half of my life was the complete opposite and relationships always came way before the task.) Mostly I get on with my work—writing has saved me from going crazy. I write every day, finishing a book that's been coming along for three years now.

July is coming closer when I go to Italy for the first time to present a paper at the Science and Nonduality conference up in the beautiful Italian hills. This has become my pilgrimage and I've been looking forward to it all year, arranging the year around it. I'm excited and nervous. I don't speak Italian except for food, buongiorno and arrivederci, so I've no idea how I'll manage. The conference is a gift to myself, a week of spiritual and scientific ideas and people. My paper is a gift I bring to the conference community—I "go beyond myself" as the two Irish masters say.

So, I walk on, still swamped by giant waves of sadness. Less frequently now.

Walk On

Pilgrims walk this path
shimmering and mystical
then clouded and dark
or hidden in veils of sorrow.

Moonshine silvers the world
with glistening tears of love
in awe of ancient ancestors
we walk on to our creation.

Falling Away

Looking back later, I experienced a "falling away" during the intense months of grief, for me the first year. It's difficult to explain any other way than falling away. I hope you might know intuitively what this means or will understand it as I explain further.

Everything extraneous—many things familiar, things I wanted but were now not possible, what didn't matter anymore or on my own again lacked sufficient meaning to continue ... all these things and actions fell away. I let them all go. I must have grieved for them too because there is the sense of loss. One of the biggest things was selling the farm and moving away from the country, from the life we had there, from friends and neighbours. The only way to cope was to accept and let go. When I was much younger I'd try to hang on to the essence of what must change, bringing mementoes that I did not have room for. Things and mementoes served to weigh me down and prolong heartache and futility. Everyone in the family must let go and let things fall away. Memories will always be with us.

With that came a feeling of laying myself bare, of being lighter too and living life in a pure and less complicated way. Now I live a different life. It is smaller, contracted. Conversely, in some ways life is more expansive too, with more presence for instance, and attention to what I give and create. Is it better or worse? That is not the question. It is different. There's the same sunset and sunrise, the same beautiful night sky, I am the same self, but there is a different landscape I walk in.

So the inner landscape as well as the outer landscape have changed. For better or worse? Who knows? I set out to enjoy my self, to find some belonging in new communities. I wonder if after the time of falling away I am left freer, more able to be and do what I find transcendent, beautiful. It hope that is the way it is.

Losing my husband and his absence from my life, forced me to accept the reality of life fallen away, the end of our era together. There is nothing else to do. There is no going back. Clinging to the past only tries to prevent the natural movement that will not be prevented. I need to move into the next season and the next phase of the moon: they come along, anyway. It is unpreventable. I seem to be okay. Then out of the blue I am thrown back to feel heartache and loss.

I wonder if it's the same for you.

Journal Note

Sometimes I feel lost. I dismay of where I am in life. I have regrets about what has brought me here, about choices made or the way I managed difficulties. I notice it is times of suffering as well as happiness that bring me back home, sometimes after years of wandering down paths taking me to what turned out to be dead ends. I call on my Zen witness for help and guidance. Is this a part of my soul I turn to? Or just a better intelligence with a better perspective? Then I remember where I am going and what I have promised myself. For what I promise myself is a promise to others as well. They are the beneficiaries of my promises.

Pilgrim's Steps

It is said that sorrow is a river and grief is an ocean. We have descended to the depths and felt the full weight of our loss. We have stood in the fire of grief, alive to heartbreak until slowly, slowly, the inner flames died down. This is a long pilgrimage which can only be done by taking heart and courage. And that's what we do.

We can't stop clinging to memories straight away. We need time before we are ready. Once we are ready enough—not fully ready — then we can take a small step forward. Just the next step, not a leap or anything too big. Later, another step. Slow movements, not back to life because we have never left life, but on in life. Then we get a little lighter and lighter every day. Ultimately and given time, we rekindle the fire of our own spirit, so that our life energy returns. The Phoenix rises.

A Pilgrim's Question

What is the one
question
that persists
that has been
with you
all along?

A companion
question
that underlies
your life
like a vein of
gold
in the earth
of your being.

Invoke and savour
that question.
Let go
the answer.
Let go
the lesser
questions, the ones
that invoke
the smaller self.

Find your
companion
question, the one
that underlies
your life
like the
dazzling
vein of gold
deep
in the earth
of your being.

III | Living Without Them

The Third Threshold:
Beauty

The Task of the third threshold, Beauty, is to live life without our loved-one. While that is the task, the means is seeing beauty. Beauty frames and fortifies this ongoing task and provides a connection between soul and meaning. To live well and fully for the rest of our life, it is central to cultivate soul and meaning. Love, wellbeing, purpose and belonging are able to grow from this fertile soil. The best way I know to enrich the soil of our being is through the daily practice of seeing beauty, because it reflects the sweetness of life and human nature.

At this threshold we encounter unexpected moments and unanticipated gifts that remind us of the mystery of being and that we are part of the wonder of life being made manifest. The terrain we walk is a reflection of our inner world and what we see externally reflects who and what we are internally. As grief eases, we continue as pilgrims through the landscape of our hearts and mind. When we set an intention to see beauty externally, we set an intention for our inner state to be beautiful. We see beauty around us and in others and enjoy the opportunity to renew and heal ourselves. If we embrace what is required of us at this threshold, we have limitless opportunity to see and embody beauty.

Once the descent into the soulwork of grieving is underway and healing begun, the Phoenix rises from the ashes. We go on living without our beloved, though they remain in our heart and mind forever. Each one of us will step through the third threshold to a life without them. We have a choice as to what that life will be like. We can choose to move away from the darkness of our descent into grief, and back into the ascent to light. Step by step, we recover from the inside out to take our place again in the world. Sometimes it is a new place.

Chapter 11

Seeing Beauty

I am doing an apprenticeship in beauty, to see beauty on a daily basis in the ordinary everyday, as well as in what takes my breath away because it is so beautiful and astonishing. Sunrises and sunsets do it every time. I'm actively bringing more beauty into my life. I know that when I see, hear and touch beauty there can be no angst or darkness and while sense of loss and sadness remains, without fear or anger there is a beauty to sadness too.

Seeing beauty is transcendent. Like kindness, beauty is powerfully transformative. The beauty I'm talking about is different to looking beautiful or having something beautiful. *Seeing beauty is a state of mind*, a way of seeing the world with an intent of wonder and an outcome of healing. To see the beauty all around uplifts the soul. To me, beauty is the enabler and hastener of recovery.

We have all become good at being critical of our surroundings and our circumstances (well, I'm good at it). The politics we hear everyday is largely criticism, and much of life is made negative and dramatised on the news; after all, what people fear and are concerned about is what sells news. Negativity becomes the way we attune our ear. Many humans are aware of this, that it is difficult to feel gratitude or generosity with a negative outlook and bleak stories running in the background — or front of mind for that matter.

Beauty. The word carries its own cliché due to the way it is used interchangeably with glitz and sex. Sexiness and glamour are ideals and benchmarks that change over time. The ideals have been imposed and are beyond the reach or sustainability for most as mere mortals.

There is a different way to see beauty. In *The Symposium,* Plato spoke of devotion to beauty including physical beauty, explaining that beauty depends on its goodness and ethical significance. Along similar lines that take us away from commercial beauty, I'm drawn to the interpretation of the Irish poet and scholar, John O'Donohue:

"Beauty is that, in the presence of which, we feel more alive".

How beautiful and simple is that? O'Donohue is pointing to the relationship being the key to beauty, one to invoke a quality of aliveness in us, and the relationship can be to a person, to nature, a place, an artwork or an animal. Beauty engages our spirit. This is true whether the beauty we see is in a human face or the sound of a voice, in the dewdrops on a spider's web, beautiful music, or a twilight sky of stars. Then to top it all, there are a handful people we meet in a lifetime, when our soul flourishes and dances and we become more in their company.

That is what I believe John O'Donohue was getting at. Consider it for a moment . . . If we feel more alive in the presence of beauty, then there is a dynamic and revitalising relationship going on between us and with what we see, feel or hear as beautiful.

To see beauty, there must be a *willingness* to see beauty, to enter into relationship and accept its truth, feel its unique presence. This takes us beyond our selves and into the realm of awe and mystery. Certainly to the realm of wonderment. Beauty engages heart and mind and elevates the heart-mind to new levels of being as Rumi knew, sometimes with ecstasy:

"The only lasting beauty is the beauty of the heart."

I like the notion of beauty growing out of the muck. It is an analogy behind the Buddhist lotus flower symbol. Along similar lines with a stretch of the imagination, I coined a phrase to use with private clients, that all gardeners will understand the significance of straight away. It is, "Turn the shit into fertiliser", a task we all must do, turn our false assumptions and negativity into what is our truth. With good fertiliser we get good growth and then good nourishment—but in order to make fertiliser we must start with the waste material and tend to its transmutation.

Seeing Beauty

It's impossible to be consumed by negative emotion
when you can see beauty all around you.
Many people do not see beauty
but constantly seek it, chase after it.

Actively appreciating the beauty
in front of your eyes will elevate beauty
to the centre of consciousness
creating delight and wonder.

Then something magical starts to occur—
Life gets better.
— Excerpt from *The Power of Place*, 2010

If you feel unloved or can't find love in your heart for someone, whether they are young or old, stop trying to find love. Instead, *look at the beauty all around*—in nature, in the stars and moonlight, in words, the human touch, and all the effort put into making the world safe and healing. Look at the faces of the humans in your life and know there is an entire life story of care and heartbreak that has sculpted every one.

Love is an experience and beauty is the context. Beauty in some form is always present with love, the fabric of human life. We can evolve past fear and suffering when we *engage* with beauty. When we open up to beauty, renewal becomes a response. We celebrate life.

The grief pilgrimage primes us for the joy of beauty. Let it do its work to help us evolve and rather than try to scurry back to the way things were. Anyway, we know that is not possible because our loved-one is not there. Life is forever changed. Instead, as we make our life one of seeing beauty, then with it comes more and more beautiful experiences. A beautiful life—not for you alone but for who you are in the world and for those you love—is the greatest gift you can give.

Beauty as a State of Mind

In the midst of recovering from grieving and slowly going forward with life, try putting thoughts of beauty at centre mind. Seeing beauty is a way to set things right for the day. On waking each morning, make sure there is something you love or find beautiful to open your eyes to. A flower, a branch of fragrant pine, a lovely image, a piece of special music, or a garment of clothing. Whatever is beautiful to you. When you place it in your room the previous night, do so with care and set the intent of waking to something beautiful to start the next day.

Recalling that beautiful image, sound or object throughout the day is like returning home. When you face undesired aspects or difficulties of the day like meeting others who are stressed and don't treat you well, or you may not treat others well yourself, in your mind return home to your symbol of beauty. Rest there for a moment. Feel your breathing. Know that seeing beauty is replenishing your soul. No matter what goes on in the external world, know you can always create these small moments of grace for some shelter and revival.

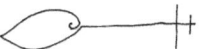

Seeing beauty around us and in others is one thing. We can learn to see beauty in our self as well and in our experience of grief and loss. Even if it is many years since the death of your loved-one, it is never too late to make the ending and loss into a beautiful ending. Beauty is a state of mind with a relational and healing intent and it can be cultivated. **We weave a beautiful ending together from threads of hope, courage, love and plain basic wilfulness.** It is an approach that gently wraps us in the silken fabric of our recovery and healing breath.

Beautiful endings arise out of great loss and heartbreak. You can have loss and grief on its own without making it a beautiful ending, but not the other way around, a beautiful ending without the grief and heartbreak. A beautiful ending is always created out of grief, no matter what the practicalities and quality of the ending was like. A beautiful ending is an inner process; it creates the last harvest of all that has gone into your relationship with the one who has died. All the accumulated goodness is concentrated within us now. We reap the harvest of our relationship through memories and gratitude, and the beautiful ending starts to form.

Paradoxically, grief can bring us to a beautiful place within, to embody transcendence and oneness. It is not pain free, yet a beautiful ending is embraced.

Falling Leaves

I loved living on the farm because I was tuned into the changing of the seasons. I find all the seasons beautiful. Martin died in late autumn, and as the season changed to winter the European trees lost the last of their coloured leaves, leaving the branches bare and stark in the cold. But when I looked close-up at the branches, from where each leaf had fallen I could already see emerging a tiny bud getting ready for new spring life. That simple observation had been completely overlooked every other year. Now it seemed almost sacred. It gave me hope and a feeling of sad joy.

These are the unpredictable moments of grace. Going through the loss and intensity of the ending with the repeated confrontation of non-permanence and letting go of all that was, has simultaneously highlighted its opposite. An appreciation of what is now, being in the cycles and magic of life. I encourage and develop this appreciation to help me recover and heal. With appreciation comes wonder, mystery and beauty, and with that, remembering who I really am and why I am here.

Chapter 12

Healing, an Ancient Art

Healing is an ancient art. When we have been in the grip of grief we can be blind and deaf to the healing we need. We can prepare to accept the healing as it is offered by being alert and non-defensive, even when the treatment is a bitter pill. Although healing and recovery is a process that is sensitive and emotional, we are capable and aware enough as adults to discern if the pill is meant as a cure or a spite, and to swallow the healing pill for its power to help.

When Healing is a Bitter Pill

The following story is one of healing and shows the path to healing, which is why it is told at this stage of the book. Although the story content takes us back to the dying journey where it is set, the message is what's important: to get out of our own way and accept healing when it is offered. We can be blind to the ways we prevent our own healing, even with the good intention of doing the best thing. Sometimes healing comes from unexpected sources, surprising us and taking us off guard. It is easy to be defensive to healing gifts and protective of our selves at this time, to miss the helping hands along the way, hands that sometimes hold out a bitter pill for us to take.

Cara's world revolves around her son. Cara is a computer programmer living a comfortable life with her only child, twelve-year-old Ben. As a single mother at nearly fifty, her life is well organised and she can afford not to work if she chooses after receiving an inheritance. Her parents died within eight months of each other, leaving everything to her as their sole child.

Ben is friendly, funny and outgoing, the sort of kid everyone at school wants to have on their team. At the school, Cara is in everything possible for parents to be involved in, and her friends consist of the parents of his friends.

One cold winter morning Ben is late getting out of bed. He doesn't respond to Cara's calls to get up. Annoyed, Cara thinks he's been up far too late playing computer games again and now she will be late for work. Cara runs upstairs to Ben's room. "Ben! Still in bed! Come on, get up, you lazy thing." But Ben doesn't make any moves to get up. Cara stalks over, ready to pull off the bedclothes. She sees his face is in a pool of vomit. As Ben tries to respond to her, Cara stands stock still. Something is terribly wrong. Ben's speech is garbled and confused. He seems to be paralysed down his left side. "Don't worry Ben-sweet. I'll get help." Cara races downstairs for her phone and dials emergency.

After hours of medical tests and scans, Ben is diagnosed with a brain tumour. It takes Cara a long time for the facts to sink in. The doctors are initially elusive, unwilling to commit to saying anything definite. Further tests happen over the next day. Eventually they say the tumour is aggressive and inoperable right now. It could be terminal. Time will tell.

She quits her job and spends every day in hospital with Ben. Her emotions rise. Her nights are frantic and sleepless. Cara becomes wracked with anxiety, tormented and unable to function rationally. Her exhaustion amplifies her emotional state. She fears Ben will die and fears he will suffer. She fears for herself, and the massive, unthinkable loss of her only child. Who will she be she without him?

Fears take over her life and contaminate the time she spends with Ben. As the days go by, she babbles on to him about incidentals, details and even gossip, trying to do her best to cheer him up. Finally, Ben blurts out in his slurred voice, "Stop it! Or go away. You're always so worried about everything, mum. All the things that don't matter. Why can't you just be with me? I'm the one who's dying!" Cara stands staring at Ben, no tears, frozen and scarcely breathing. She stops herself from saying, "How can you think you're dying?" realising the truth in it. Her face reddens and burns as she realises a nurse is in the room and heard it all.

Cara decides to seek help. She goes to her old doctor, Lynda. Now retired, Lynda has become a friend after knowing Cara for thirty-five years. Cara gives Lynda all the medical information she has and recounts Ben's words. Lynda is quiet, then has a different view of things.

"Can you accept the healing message in Ben's words, Cara?" Cara looks blank. "Your fears have taken you away. They've put a barrier between you and your child. This is the time that he needs you most. You and Ben are being robbed of the precious time you have left together.

With this bitter medicine, Cara finds it in herself to become present with Ben. By just being there for him, she can love her son while he is still alive. To her surprise, her panic calms as some equanimity is restored, and she redirects her attention away from herself, toward Ben. She learns to see, hear, feel, laugh, cry and respond to him in the moment. Rather than a slap in the face, the words from Ben become a healing gift that stays with her for life.

Wishing and Hoping

Part of grieving that some humans experience is magical thinking about the loved-one who has died. Part of recovery is either stopping the magical thinking or understanding it is wishful thinking that will not actually happen. **Magical thinking is the persistent *wish and hope* that our loved-one will come back,** and one day they will return to us. Ideas and images go on in the mind that we don't tell anyone about because we know they are irrational. However, irrational does not mean these thoughts and imaginings are not powerful and persistent. For instance, thinking our loved-one is not really dead, the whole thing is a pretence for some reason and one day they will walk back in through the front door and explain all. The idea I had from the time I was eight years old when my father died, was although he was dead, he watched everything I did — and this was not good for a mischievous girl that relished playing risky tricks on her teachers; and it only got worse as a teenager and young adult! I believed when people died their spirit stayed around and was all-seeing. This belief went in and out of awareness, initially dominating my thoughts when I was a child, and later on, there only sporadically.

Finally, I expelled these thoughts completely, but before that I carried the strange burden for two decades. I did not know what I was doing was magical thinking nor that it is quite a common part of grief, for people of any age. I wonder if it is when we stop wishing and hoping we are able to say the final goodbye to the over-one. What do you think? Having eventually got "rid of my ghosts" and wishful magical thinking by saying a heart felt goodbye, it never bothered to revisit me during all the subsequent deaths and grieving encountered.

Magical thinking is different in nature and quality to other activities, like when we adopt our passed loved-one's point of view and step into their shoes to investigate a problem . For instance, we might have a "discussion" with our dead loved-one about something significant, when we know full well they are not really there, nevertheless we reply to ourselves in the way they would have replied to us or given advice.

Recovery

We need to grieve our loss. Then we need to recover and heal. As human beings, we all have the capacity to be the conductor of the winds that blow through our life. An impossible task? Not when we go into the task of the conductor, which is to get the best music from all that is available. Waiting for the best musicians and the best conditions to come along could mean waiting a long, long time.

Having a loved-one die is a long and deep immersion into grieving. Grief happens, whether or not it was a good death, and whether or not your life went back to the normal day to day soon afterwards or was never the same again. For some, going back to work or the usual routine is enormously helpful, for others it is the last thing they want to do, and for some it is just not a possibility. We all deal with our grief individually and according to what circumstances demand.

There comes a time for healing and recovery. It is part of our life task to heal and return our innate goodness to the world. This is born out by the etymology of the word *heal*, literally "to make whole." The root of *recovery* is from the Anglo-French meaning "return to health". The notion is to **return to health and reclaim being whole.** The alternative is to be windblown every which way, pushed and pulled by the forces of circumstance, expectation, and the external environmental pressures we live in.

At first, grief is like looking back on all that is lost and gone while reluctantly looking forward to what might be. Sometimes there is blank bewilderment about what to make of the life stretching ahead with whatever time that we have left. How could anything worthwhile follow on from this?

Helpful Words from Science and Buddhism

For centuries, Buddhists and other contemplary practices from many religions and disciplines have reported that stilling the mind and centring the self as a regular practice reaps great benefit. During the last few decades neuroscience added its voice with scientific research and evidence to prove this is so. **Neuroplasticity has proved that the mind can consciously engage in shaping itself.**

In the last three decades, neuroscience has caught up with spiritual teachings by researching wellbeing and happiness. Neoroscience turned its sights beyond remedial aspects of shaping the mind, such as reducing depression or regaining lost limb movement, and toward building positive psychological conditions for living.

Canadian neuroscientist, Richard Davidson, met the Dalai Lama in 1992. The Dalai Lama challenged Davidson, saying, "You've used your tools to study fear, anxiety, depression. Why can't you use those same tools to study kindness and compassion?" Davidson was struck to the core by this. He immersed himself in Buddhist teachings and remains a devoted practitioner and friend of the Dalai Lama. Subsequently he realigned his work to develop a theory of wellbeing, and built the Centre for Healthy Minds at the University of Wisconsin. Davidson's findings are available on YouTube and he is a joy, saying, "Wellbeing is a skill," and our brain and genomics are not fixed as previously thought. Instead there is much plasticity including the growth of new brain cells, and there are bi-directional highways between the brain and the body. His research concluded that **ongoing wellbeing is influenced by four brain circuits.** In summary they are:

> **Our ability to recover from negative states.** Apart from being in a generally positive state, we can succumb to negative states and get stuck there.
>
> **Our ability to maintain positive states** or see the world from a positive disposition, experiencing positive emotions.

Our ability to be generous. Yes, an entire brain circuit devoted to generosity. Generosity and compassion generate good feeling that rebounds.

Our ability for focus and avoid mind-wandering. This is the specific ability meditation aims to develop and what we tap into when we're in "flow".

The four together generate wellbeing and components of grief recovery. In my book, seeing beauty will aid and enable all four states. There comes a time for the constancy of mourning to end. Restoring wholeness and aliveness is the aim after grieving for the loss of a loved-one.

Three Principles of Recovery

The first principle is: Be ready.
Recovery happens in your own time and not according to any pre-determined customs or rules. You know when you are ready because you want to start doing things and seeing people again. Your interests return a little at first, and you start to wonder how friends, family or community members are, want to say hello and make contact, even if only briefly at first.

The second principle is: Rise above fear.
Fear serves to pull us away from our meaning in life. Fear either fragments our thoughts and confuses, or has us fixated on only one thing that we perceive as threatening, ignoring everything else that counterbalances the threat.

For decades I've been regarding fear as the polarity of love: Fear and love, one being the antithesis of the other. But there is another paradigm that is also useful to consider:

Fear—Growth

Fear—growth and fear—love are both powerful to think of as pathways. We reach a fork in the path and must make a choice. One path is fear. The other path is growth (or love). We are not simply victims to our emotions such as fear, because emotions come and go. They have been described as e-motions because they are always in motion. E-motions rise and fall in intensity and in our attention. We are not victims of our emotions, helpless in the wake of life events or forces that stir a fear response and cause us to be swept along by them. Fear rises up, and if we do not feed it, it falls away. Like any emotion or physiological response they are not naturally sustained. Emotions come and go, rise and fall in intensity. Let fear subside and be overcome by growth and curiosity.

The third principle is: Find meaning.
Humanistic psychologist Abraham Maslow developed a theory of higher order values he called "Being-Values". They are over-arching core values such as wholeness, justice, love, goodness, beauty and truth. For each of us there is a meta-value, one that stands head and shoulders above the others and is a theme running through our life. That meta-value, once we identify it, is our conductor. It naturally facilitates 'right' behaviours that are perfectly congruent with our being-value.

Unlike other species, as homo sapiens we developed the mind as our major survival characteristic. In fact, the capacity of our brain far exceeds what was needed for our survival alone. To satisfy our mind, we turned it to learning, exploring, investigating, discovering and inventing. Therefore, it is a matter of what we learn from a fear or grief experience as an example, and what it means that is of central importance. How we use the learning and meaning leads to growth.

Growth as Intent

We navigate life with one of two basic mindsets: fixed and growth, according to the best selling author Carol Dweck, in her book on mindset. A fixed mindset is seeing the way things are as permanent, including our own intelligence, personality and relationships. A growth mindset is seeing we can cultivate our life and our qualities through our efforts and learning: and I add, through the meaning we give to what happens to us. If we choose an intention of growth and pursue it instead of staying fixed and feeling stuck, then we start to be freed up. When we are freer, transformative things start to happen. A mindset of growth in relation to something we fear, for instance, helps us rise above it, whereas a fixed mindset of the fear or its object, is permanent. An intention of growth helps shift us out of fear and other states, including grief.

Deepening Consciousness

Grief is a pilgrimage involving suffering and holds a powerful potential—the experience of transformation. As part of the spiritual and emotional pilgrimage especially over the first twelve months or so, I felt like a trapdoor in my mind had opened and dropped me down to a new level of consciousness. Others say they experienced a similar deepening and advancement of consciousness as the outcome of grief.

Throughout this companion book, grief has been explored from the overlapping frames of the personal, the archetypal, and the universal plus the perspective of poets, spiritual teachers and philosophers. Stream of consciousness entries from my journal reveal some of the individual inner states as experienced at the time. I hope you have felt held as we walked through these different frames together. Although grief is a solo journey, it can't be completed alone.

Profound loss and grieving does something for us. Like a physical pilgrimage, grief is an arduous and difficult journey. It changes us. We further develop inner resources. In preparation to fully return to the community after retreat, we do well to meditate on the ways grief has changed us. The grief of losing a loved-one gives us a depth and insight not known before, such as increased perceptiveness, love, courage, connection to soul and capacity for synergy. These attributes form part of developing consciousness.

We are born with the gift of consciousness. As we evolved as humans, our consciousness became the primary survival capacity. Birds grew wings to fly, giraffes developed a long neck to reach high feed, hedgehogs grew protective quills. We developed the mind. Yet our capacity for consciousness far exceeds what is needed for survival alone. Why?

Many spiritual teachers believe that our continually evolving consciousness is why we are here and bound to keep developing toward enlightenment. We are the only species on the planet who are aware of our own development historically, socially and personally, and who work out the evolution of the planet and other celestial bodies in the universe. Personal and universal evolving consciousness moves us toward higher consciousness and oneness. Along the way we get to know our true gift personally to make our contribution to others and as part of humanity. Rumi demonstrates the intent so elegantly in these few lines:

Be a lamp, or a lifeboat, or a ladder.

Help someone's soul heal.

Walk out of your house like a shepherd.

Whatever pathway we choose, we can walk it like a shepherd and help someone's soul heal. We do our own soulwork, have been through grief conditions that deepen our consciousness and awareness, and we intimately know suffering and compassion.

We become more receptive to others suffering. Grief takes us to the underground river of the collective soul and consciousness, where innate wisdom bubbles up. This is humbling. As one of the biggest life experiences, grief matures us. Through personal suffering we become more aware of universal suffering, of the time we spontaneously go inward, seek solitude and need to enquire, explore. In my twenties after I had grieved the death of a friend,

I described grief leaving me with a shift to see the world in vivid colour with new depth and contrast. Grief expands our sensitivity and a range of human perceptions that otherwise we may not notice. In grief we are more empathic to others vulnerability and pain in all its forms.

This opening out is a precursor to further developing consciousness. We are primed. Insights are opened up in ways we would not normally notice. We may recognise a great deal about our selves and our lives, including the way we see the world and the way our mind works. The words of the Greek playwright, Aeschylus, ring out from 458 BC, "We suffer into truth."

The Alchemy of Suffering

Whatever way we live our lives, all of us harbour times when we symbolically stand in the fire, the inner fire of suffering. When we don't run away from the heat and its burning, surprisingly it is tolerable, and beyond becomes transformational. The fire within is part of an inner alchemical process that Jung spoke of at length as a metaphor for personal transformation, which he called "calcinatio". As we face the inner burning we become more aware of what is happening as it unfolds and what alchemists call "a secret fire". It is a flame of life, the instinctual urge for growth and transformation awakened through grief. The alchemical metaphor reflects the process of personal transformation and can be regarded as a system of self-initiation.

Many of the great philosophers and psychotherapists believed that suffering has an alchemical-like effect that we are conscious of—alchemy being the metaphor for personal transformation. Frankl was clear it was one of the three ways we create meaning out of whatever life brings. With meaning and therefore purpose in life, we are capable of self-actualising and the stage beyond for some, of reaching a state of self-transcendence. Just as trees such as eucalypts and redwoods need fire to release their seeds, do we need suffering the inner fire for new growth and to release meaning and our opus, our life's work?

Chapter 13

Wise Life Guides

There are two special wise life guides I'd like to draw your attention to. The first is an archetype in the form of the mythological Roman god, Janus. Archetypes represent the shared universal patterns underlying thought, behaviours and forming values and other characteristics of humanity, that are ingrained and have been passed down through the ages and the collective unconscious. Well known examples of archetypes are the Warrior, the Innocent, the Wise Old Woman, and the Healer.

The other wise life guide I want to mention is Death as a life companion. Staying aware that our time on Earth is limited, over too soon, and that death can come to anyone at any time including you and me, we are inclined to sharpen discernment about what really matters in life, who we love, where we are going and how we are living. The the inevitability of our own death becomes a teacher for the way to live life and heightens awareness of the way we treat others. We cannot forget that this is not a one way street, in that the way we treat our selves is reflected in relationships. To be integrated, in other words, the kindnesses we extend to others, we also extend to our selves.

Janus, the Archetype

There is an ancient archetype that depicts exactly what it is like to be in this state of beginning recovery from grief and loss. The archetype is part of our shared humanity that dates back to 27 BC. Janus epitomises being right in the middle of the liminal position and the core dilemma of being at the threshold that marks a major ending and a beginning. Beginnings always contain unknowns even when we think they don't.

Endings and Beginnings

Janus is the patron of beginnings and endings. Amongst the ancient Roman gods, Janus was the guardian god of doors, thresholds, gates and bridges. (Other Indo-European cultures, as well as ancient Mesopotamia, also had deities with two faces according to Wiley's online library.) The name Janus comes from the Latin *Ianus*, literally meaning a "gate, arched passageway". The month of January is from the Latin *Ianuarius* meaning the month of Janus. According to the early Romans it was the month that was sacred as the beginning of the year.

Janus is the Roman god that has come to be known as having two faces—one looking back, the other looking forward. The ancient statues and images show Janus with both faces, one in front, the other at the back, looking both forwards and backwards. In modern times, Janus has earned himself a bad name that is undeserved, with "being two-faced" sometimes connected with being deceitful in our culture. However, deceit is far from the original meaning of having two faces.

Janus was the protector of crossings and transition. He held the bridge from one part of life to the next and was regarded as the guardian to the gates of heaven. He was always indelibly linked to the seasons as one followed the other.

It is believed the two faces of Janus also represented looking to the east and the west, to sunrise and sunset. These two horizons are where we experience the birth and end of each day as it comes and goes. It is a fitting metaphor for our own lives. Jungian psychology links the east with rising consciousness and the west with the ever-present depths of the unconscious; both integral to our wellbeing, with the tension between them creating life and energy.

As we look to the east and the west of our life, can we regard the liminal threshold of living without the one we held dear as a sacred passage? With the death of someone close, more than at any other time, we become open to the spiritual, our consciousness and the beautiful mystery of life and death.

Reflecting on grieving after the death of her father, Mari spoke to me of her experience: "I felt that the change was like crossing a bridge over a big canyon. Then the bridge burned. There was no way back but I sat and looked out backwards with the shock of it anyway, for 6 months or so. Then timing dictated I would get up and go. I realised further on when reading the section here on Janus that I was in this threshold space all that time, the six months—consoled by your words that this may take a long time. Joni Mitchell's song comes to mind here, *I've looked at life from both sides now.*"

Timing is a divine healer for grief. Somehow, looking both backward and forward is important to keep doing and "here you'll stay until it's time for you to go", in Buffy Sainte-Marie's wistful words of love. Then you find at last you take some forward steps.

Death as a Life Companion

What we know for certain about death is everyone will die and we don't know when. A reminder of our own death is a ritual some people do daily, like the refrain from American Pie, "Today is the day I might die". The purpose of a daily reminder is to refresh an appreciation for life.

Ancient societies commonly have some version of death as a friend or advisor, for example, imagining death like a tiny person who sits on your left shoulder as a trusted guide and friend. Death's job is to open up your appreciation of life and sharpen awareness, so that the ordinary and everyday are noticed and savoured along with the more profound. Instead, the ordinary becomes special, significant. We see the significance in others, our friends and those around us. People who know they are dying say they see life again through fresh eyes, and the unnecessary noise of life such as defeatist self-talk falls away, so they are left with a pure sense of life and all that is wonderful.

Why wait until you're dying, when this could be available to you right now?

The awareness and acceptance of death plays a part in how well we heal. Going through the death of a loved-one is deeply confronting, leading us to question the meaning of life and, in particular, the meaning of our own life. It is natural to contemplate death and dying during grief and wonder about what really happens at the moment of death and afterward. Thinking about our own death inevitably comes up.

Confronting death is especially frightening for young people. As we age, there is more acceptance of death and gratitude for life. As we become more accepting, we're able to find happiness in what is, instead of hankering after what is not and what we wish for. A bigger and richer perspective is born as a door opens to appreciating what we have. The conversation about how precious something is after it has been lost is embodied when absence teaches us the value and significance of its presence, our loved-one just as is, with all imperfections. Philosopher Costica Bradatan puts it so succinctly, "Life needs death for reasons of self-realisation". In his book, *Dying for Ideas*, Bradatan considers how philosophers look at death, how death looks at philosophers, and realising death is more than thoughts and words—it is an embodiment made visible through actions and expression.

Death remains a known unknown and one of life's greatest mysteries. Even after many soulful and sad goodbyes, death continues to fill me with awe and wonder. The way we regard death and approach it has a large bearing on the experience we will have of dying. Religions teach this. If the circumstances of dying are extreme such as a prolonged illness, we still have choice in our frame of mind and attitude. I hope to approach my death with calm, love and curiosity. To urge this along, I imagine my best experience of dying. It is a rehearsal. With only one go at dying, I don't want to mess it up. Dying is the ultimate transition and death the final transformation—such a precious passage. Our bodies become ashes or fodder for the earth while our souls become stardust.

Life Needs Death for Reasons of Self-Realisation

Since dying is the ultimate endpoint of life, why not treat it as a goal? Why not have a vision? Soulwork about our immortality reconnects with our source. That reconnection is calming and accentuates the positives; then we are able to make better sense of living and dying.

When we realise our own life is limited we are compelled to treat it wisely. Fears of death need to be released. Our responsibilities, lifestyle, goals and contemplation can be integrated and attuned with heart and soul. New ways to live the same life with meaning, purpose and currents of happiness can be explored with more understanding of what is meant by "death is the great companion" and "death the good friend". It is not morbid. It is life affirming.

The story of the chrysalis is a superb allegory for emerging from grief. After growing into a strong caterpillar, time is up for that part of life. The caterpillar spins a cocoon around itself. Inside, it liquifies and disintegrates. Then cells that have been dormant wake up and start to reform. Over a long period for a chrysalis, a new form develops until finally, the adult butterfly hatches, stretches out wings for the first time ever, and flies away. It has gone through an extreme transformation and emerged thousands of times more evolved than its previous self.

This is what grief can do.

Grief takes us deeply inside our self. It is usual to "cocoon" and want time alone, sheltered from the world. We feel as though we're disintegrating, whereas it's an aspect of our life that has disintegrated. We get caught up thinking we should be in control, yet to strive for control does not do us any good. The control is an illusion and we have no control over loss or grief, just acceptance and then adaptation.

We have the meltdown inside our cocoon and express grief in all its forms. Innately, we know instinct will lead the way. And it does. The reservoir of inner resources that have been lying dormant come to life. Ultimately, we become ready to emerge into the world again.

We Don't Need to Wait Until We Die to Transform

Start now. Life can be about *living well* not only *living without* them. Holding back from living well for whatever reason will ensure ongoing misery. There is no betrayal in going on to have some fulfilment and joy in life and would be what your loved-one wants for you. While this makes sense, I still grappled with it in the back of my mind. Who was I to live while he had died? I have talked with others at a loss to know what to do: either nothing seems to appeal to living well, or they *think about* it but are not trying anything out. Life is going to be different without your loved-one there and it's up to us to accommodate it.

No matter what your relationship with the loved-one, a life partner, child, parent, friend, life still holds meaning and enjoyment for you. Feeling disinterested, unmotivated, lethargic, anxious or stuck are symptoms of grief. Irritation, self-doubt and confusion can plague us. One of the best antidotes I know is to *experiment with new things and actively become curious*, in particular, things that get you up and out. I'm a lover of forests, rivers, mountains, valleys and oceans—any beautiful landscape and skyscape, so those are where I head. If I can't get out to the country I go to the most beautiful park I can find, and we are blessed with magnificent public parks and gardens in my city. I am happy to do this on my own but for company there are walking groups available in most cities and towns. New experiences and visiting new places summon renewal and revitalisation. The quality of life improves. We don't need a grand plan before doing anything. We just need to start getting out there.

A quick word about the mind and perception in the context of healing and going on to living life with your loss.

The principles at the centre of neuroscience, spirituality and the wisdom traditions contain enduring truths about humanity. Expressed differently, these truths have the same message: healer, heal thyself (relevant even if you're not considering becoming a healer).

Left to its own devices, the mind can play tricks on us, like thinking the past is the present. The Irish have a saying they relish for its contradiction:

"The thing about the past is it is not really the past."

This notion is found in Gestalt therapy and other existential psychotherapies: our past wounds are present in the body-heart-mind and affect us in the present until we become aware of what is going on, memory by memory. The indicator of past wounding is essentially our emotions, particularly a propensity for a strong emotional reaction such as defensiveness, anger, tears, or envy etc.

Indigenous traditions caution against assumptions and thoughts that prevent and block healing and self-awareness. Teaching is given during life transition passages, especially to early adults undergoing the vision quest. According to cultural anthropologist Angeles Arrien, the life teachings from a Native American tribe (see Mills and Sparks) take the form of being made aware of these eight false assumptions:

If only—Someone close to me hadn't died, or I were rich, or I were famous, or I could find the right person to marry, or I had more friends, or I were more attractive, or I weren't disabled in any way, or the world were a better place—Then I would be happy.

Each of these false beliefs points attention in the wrong direction, outward instead of inward.

By recognising the past wounding and tending to healing with love and care, we make sense of what happened in a new way and are able to tell a new story about what occurred. Until then, the injury and the energy it carries remain the *living* past, here in our present and projecting on into our future.

The Healing Practices numbers 15 to 20 in Part IV will help, and Chapter 6, Soulwork. Healing has a bearing on going forward and the future life we make in the absence of our loved-one. With healing we are free to change perspective of what happened in the past and what may happen in the future (for example from pessimistic to a life-affirming perspective) and heal what occurs in our body-heart-mind.

Setting out again is hard. Taking the first step out of grief and loss is the biggest. It is not like any other beginning in its painfulness. A new beginning starts when you feel your spirit start to rise again and gently take you out of your gloom. It's like rising from some dark, greedy earth that wants to suck you back to its depths. But something in you resists. Something in you knows it is time, whether it has been weeks, months or years, and for your own sake you must now make your way ahead. Slowly, slowly, you pull yourself up and out again into a world of light. You start to return in full to the community.

Out of Grief

The biggest step is the first out of grief
unlike any other, not painless
your spirit gently urging
a step from greedy gloom

Something in you resists
and something in you knows
it is time now to make your way
and move slowly to a lighter world

Chapter 14

Return to the Community

After a long and intense pilgrimage through grief, there are many insights and compassionate experiences so powerful, they are sacred. Reconnection with an inner truth and our innate wisdom is not uncommon. With this reconnection still fresh and uppermost in mind, are you ready to return to the community, more evolved after your grieving pilgrimage, and give back to others? This chapter will take you through it and remind you of the territory you have covered.

From the Personal to the Universal

The grieving pilgrimage can bring us to a deep and profound knowing of all we experience as personal having a universal truth. This is significant as we move out to the community and give back to the community again in ways that are more fulfilling and mutually sustainable.

Grief is an intensely personal experience. When we don't shy away from grief and can embark on it as a pilgrimage, a sacred journey with a large inner dimension, then we find the collective experience. The deep personal immersion in grief, takes us to the realm of the universal. The specific details will always be yours and in relation to your loved-one. The experiences of the psyche and soul are universal. There is universal truth to be found there.

"We are custodians of deep and ancient thresholds," said existential philosopher, Martin Heidegger. He taught we are more than our individual experience and consciousness. We have our ancestors and the whole universe within, reflected in Rumi's beautiful words, "Do not feel lonely, the entire universe is inside you."

Keep this in your heart and mind. It can bring comfort to know you are not alone, you are walking a path of countless humans before you. It can bring courage to realise right at this moment there are many thousands going through the inner pilgrimage of grief and all it brings. It can bring nobility to know we are a microcosm of the universe.

Know grief is like a pilgrimage borne of love. We traverse through a suffering so overwhelming it envelopes us, then ends in an opening out, one of unconditional love.

Harvesting

Harvesting is the next step in soulwork, in bringing forth your gift and taking your place in the world now changed by your loss. Harvesting is releasing your song—the one you were told not to sing when you were little, the one your parents tried to protect you from so you could conform and not suffer.

Harvesting is sifting and sorting the fruits of your life. A good harvest reaps an abundance of fruits and so we share our harvest with the community. Everything about the harvest speaks of abundance, sharing and community. There is no joy in hoarding the crop ourselves.

The soulwork involved with harvesting means going into the temple of memory. Tread with care and compassion. There are surprises to be found, surprises that come from knowing your true intent, from your gifts, from grief, and always from mistakes and failure. If you do not find any mistakes or failures, look again. It is not possible to be human without them. Bring kindness and discernment to sift through your mistakes. Rather than be filled with regret and remorse, forgive. Forgive yourself and know this is part of your journey. Forgiveness frees us. Forgiveness is an act of grace.

The fruit to be harvested from forgiveness feeds the soul. Treasure the fruits you harvest, all the fruits of our life. Harvesting and sharing the abundance nourishes you internally and multiplies your capacity to nourish others.

> Something opens our wings
> something makes
> boredom and hurt disappear
> Someone fills the cup in front of us, we taste
> only sacredness
>
> *Poem from 13th century Persia, cited in Anam Cara*

At every stage of life there is the possibility of a new harvest. Each harvest will be different to any previous harvests and bring forth its own crop, just as nourishing. As we age, the harvests become increasingly abundant from when we were younger because all our losses, loves and adult aloneness gather together and deepen us. The pilgrimage of loss and suffering forms our psychospiritual development and insight. Our self-knowledge, inner resources, relationships, altruism, love and ability to contribute all deepen. Contemplated life experience reveals our truth, nourishing the harvest, feeding us and many others who need some care and shelter for a while. The Beatles said something similar and in beautifully simple words in their 1969 *Abbey Road album:*

". . . And in the end, the love you take, is equal to the love you make."

Giving and being generous is about more than giving money or time or information. It's about giving of your self. You can give time, money or information without being involved or feel anything much because it is a transaction, like paying for groceries (I agree, sometimes giving money means a great deal and is giving from the heart). Likewise, giving time to a task when it is only out of duty or what you want to get out of it for yourself has an emptiness to it. There is little joy and you and others are robbed of the benefits.

The Dalai Lama and Archbishop Desmond Tutu in their week long conversation on joy, defined as "inner joy, free of external circumstances", linked joy with generosity and purpose. Having a sense of generosity and purpose is how we contribute to others, how we feel needed by them and add value.

To give of yourself and be abundant is a heartwarming experience. Buddhism teaches there are different kinds of generosity, specifically:

> Material giving; giving freedom from fear (which involves protection, counselling or solace); and spiritual giving, which involves giving your wisdom, moral and ethical teachings, and helping people to be more self-sufficient and happier.
>
> — His Holiness the Dalai Lama.

Return to the Community

Depth mythologist and scholar, Joseph Campbell, developed the Hero's Journey. It represents the archetypal journey of humans common to cultures all over the world, down through the ages. It is built from Campbell's studies of the mythologies and cultures of indigenous and contemporary societies from all over the globe. The hero (an ancient term for leader) starts the journey by leaving the community. On the way various trials are gone through, diverse nemeses encountered, and ordeals undertaken—all to test, strengthen and develop the hero. The stakes are serious with no guarantee the hero will get out of any situations alive.

In our circumstance, the stage of significance as we recover from grief is the very last stage of the journey. It is the return to the community, a privilege and one I revere and treasure deeply. This chapter shows you why. First we'll look at the traps that block the return to the community.

The Trap

There is a trap lying on the other side of the grief threshold. I know it because I have been caught in it. Overcoming this trap is one of the defining features of recovery. The trap captures many sorts of kind, aspiring people who have much to give, but spend their time instead giving nothing.

The trap is a danger of not returning to the community. The return is the final river to cross, a challenge easily overlooked. For we don't return empty-handed; we return with a gift from our soul that we have retrieved and nurtured from the grief pilgrimage. The gift is formed by grief, like the oyster forms a pearl from inflammation around grit in its tender heart. Unless we share the gift, it remains sterile and hidden.

To refuse to return or become complacent, either way our sacred pilgrimage and gift becomes of little consequence. An inner battle with self-doubt can lead to mistrusting the gift we bring, fearing it will not be accepted and worthy. We are dismembered (metaphorically) instead of sustaining wholeness. Words of encouragement come from Ralph Waldo Emerson to do the task that now exists for our own life:

"To leave the world a bit better, whether by a healthy child, a garden patch, or redeemed social condition; to know even one life has breathed easier because you live—that is to have succeeded."

Alternatively, there can be a retreat to "the land of the lotus eaters". The place is from Greek mythology, an island that grew a mysterious lotus plant where the Greek hero, Odysseus, almost lost all his men while trying to return home. Odysseus could not return home without his men to crew the ship. Invited by the local tribe to stay and eat the lotus plant, blissful forgetfulness and complacency overcame the crew, and they refused to leave and go back to their community.

The refusal to return to the community can take the form of love or fear. Falling in love with learning, but without making a contribution to others, as an example. If all we have developed through the grieving pilgrimage becomes fragmented, split off, serving only our selves, then we stay put and do not make the final river crossing home.

Fear involves regression. We go back to the entanglement of thoughts and stories from the past that define and restrict who we are. These old stories are like continual tape loops running on and on in the background of our mind that build and reinforce self-doubt. The small self that fears will not risk possible exposure and ridicule.

The fear habit can be broken. Anthropologist and author, Carlos Castaneda, adopted a shamanic guide, Don Juan, who gave good advice:

"You talk to yourself too much. You're not unique in that. Everyone of us does. We maintain our world with our inner dialogue. A man or woman of knowledge is aware that the world will change completely as soon as they stop talking to themselves."

The deep suffering of grief interrupts the running inner dialogue and we can see ourselves and life with fresh eyes. This is the silver lining; we can wipe clean the lens we look through. Truth is perceived clearly. The soulwork digs deeply into the ground of our being. There can we find our treasure, more beautiful than a perfect flower.

I got out of the trap by considering grief as a pilgrimage. It has movements, like a musical piece, with variations of different tempos, moods, and meaning that make up the whole piece, and affect us deeply with times of hopelessness and times of beauty and the full range in between. To be immersed in the movements is physically exhausting, psychologically demanding, and completely integrating.

Having worked with Joseph Campbell's *Heroes Journey* the final stage kept coming up in my mind. The overarching themes are of separation, initiation, and return. Along the way the action parts on the road of trials, like being swallowed up and entering a dark cave, have relevance to grief. However, the recovery from grief is often overlooked and where a deeper journey begins.

The "return to the community" is taken to mean going back home, usually in a blaze of glory for Hollywood productions. But *return* has another meaning more profound and fruitful. It is to *give back* to the community. I decided, for reasons of growth, meaning and abundance, to give back and return to the community what I learned, who I am.

Grief eventually calms and eases. We have time to gather ourselves. When we are ready we return to the community not just because we need the company, because there is learning and truth to offer from standing in the fire of grief with awareness. Find out what the world needs from you now and be of service. It is service and contribution that matters, whether what you offer is humble or grand. Giving of yourself is the treasure.

Lucy started visiting old people in the home near her place to bring some warm company. Francis is a retired teacher who loves modern literature and now holds community classes in his local library. Matt, an accountant, became a volunteer football coach on weekends for the local school and his sister, Liz, started Saturday lunch BBQs to encourage parents to attend football practice for their kids. Wendy is an avid reader and started two book clubs bringing together socially isolated people. Ben decided to help out people in his neighbourhood who were elderly; he does their odd jobs on weekends plus keeps in touch to check they are okay. Robyn turned the verge in front of her house into a community vegetable garden; all welcome to help, all welcome to take what they need. Rachael got involved with her local community radio station initially helping with administration; then she trained to become a program presenter herself. Sally befriends refugees resettling and learning about a new culture.

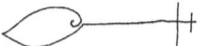

The next step is to return to the community in your imperfect, incomplete, nearly-ready, and most wonderful self (see Wabi-sabi in Part IV). Stay focussed on kindness, as the ancient Chinese philosopher Lao-Tzu advises from the sixth century BC:

> Kindness in words creates confidence. Kindness in thinking creates profoundness. Kindness in giving creates love.

We are a Work in Progress

The grief pilgrimage must come before the return. The pilgrimage is profound with threshold spaces to gather our self, transition, readjust and take up the invitation to grow. Returning to the community is *giving back* to the community and calls for giving our self, the most valuable thing we have to offer. The grief pilgrimage has meant doing soulwork and going home to our selves before returning, so our gift remains clear, meaningful and undiluted. Grief presents us with a compelling invitation to investigate and reform what is trivial and peripheral, and to find what we most value in living. We are left standing in the ground of the self and our truth with the gift we have to give.

We return to the community a work in progress, giving back.

No matter what you actually *do*, giving back is giving your goodwill, support and kindness. It is providing some human shelter to others in times of need. Taking this on does something to who we are and the way we live because there is a relationship between intent and being. It makes our life ennobled, no matter how humble.

Sometimes (possibly often) what we contribute in the end is totally different to what we believed was our forte. It has been there all the time but in the periphery of awareness. It grows clear over a lifetime. The existential philosopher and scholar, Martin Buber, put it another way,

"All journeys have secret destinations of which the traveler is unaware."

When we get into our true territory we are in harmony. There is no need to push, no need to stand back. When we hit on our gift, we know it for what it is. It is what makes us feel good, what adds value, joy and something extra to others. We can learn a lot from communities that have endured much suffering. There is a beautiful Irish proverb that the poet Padraig O'Tauma is so fond of:

"It is in the shelter of each other that the people live."

A gentle reminder that sometimes we need to shelter our fellow humans, and by so doing, we shelter ourselves.

Natural Unfolding

Build your life now without your loved-one from the ground up, the inside out, *from the inside for the outside world*. There is a natural unfolding that means doing the next little bit, not a huge leap to ten or fifty steps down the path, what I was prone do when I was younger, usually ending up in trouble. There is a next bit right ahead that is wholly different to the aspirational leap.

Sometimes we do need to make a leap as fearful and exposing as it may be. We need to take life in our hands and with all our heart, leap into the next utterance of being, without being dead sure, without having a detailed plan, no matter what or who may be left wondering. They have their own choices to make: to let you go, to make their own leap of faith into what is wholehearted for them. Or to stay where they are in life and be content with that. But leaps are either part of your DNA or not and they are not done often.

If you want to make leaps all the time to move on, you might ask why. Are you addicted to the leap, but disregard the landing and all the work that goes with it, not to mention being out of your depth. Do you like the sink or swim challenge? It sure gets the blood moving. Or are you just in a hurry? To reach a level of mastery or artistry is a long time in the making. Daniel Pink's research has found it takes at least ten thousand hours or ten years of dedicated practice and progress just to get to being good.

In that case, we progress slowly. After we master one part, we move to the bit ahead. Here it is not synonymous with your career development, although it can link and ideally it would. It is the bit ahead in soulwork, in bringing forth your gift and taking your natural place in the world. It is releasing you song—the one you were told not to sing when you were little, the one your parents tried to protect you from so you could conform and not suffer. They may have been a tad more selfish and had other motives, depending on who they were and what burdens they carried.

Just the next move. No pressure, although that is hard enough. Well, just enough pressure to get your full attention and energy levels up. It is not saying to an acorn, now be an oak tree. Even great celebrities just do what comes next and through a mix of synchronicity, readiness and opportunity, see the opportunity and act on it. Their long focus on where they are going is steadfast, unshakeable. We can do the same and the best guide I have found is seeing beauty.

The Second Surrender

The first was the time you surrendered
to that tragic knowing;
you looked it straight in the eye,
it stared back at you blankly
and you knew.
Their time has come.
Now is their turn to die.
The truth of it struck deeply
like a long dark chord within.

The second surrender wraps you
in silken threads of hope
as you walk through the doorway ahead
without them
not because you stop loving them
but because you love them still.

With gratitude for all that brought you here
you put down the weight you carry
to step lighter on along the path;
because, with it all,
part of you will find a way
to do the task you set for yourself
all those years ago
when spirits were high
and nothing seemed impossible.

The world needs aspiration. It needs evolving consciousness coming from the inside out after having suffered the descent into grief, then manifesting through contributions to others. Amazingly, these gifts become an antidote to grief and loneliness, and if you're uncertain, stop, listen, look, feel for your silken thread within.

Chapter 15

Silken Threads

The final chapter is a celebration of how precious your life is. I hope that is brought home with ever increasing meaning. The purpose of grief is not only to mourn, but also to deepen your truth. It is a form of compulsory time out to gather your love, hope and courage to go on in life without your loved-one. Know that you have said your final goodbye the best way you could and they are at rest. You too can rest from caring for them. That does not mean you stop loving them, just you are freed from responsibility. You can sleep well and the pain lessens.

There is another personal responsibility, should you choose to take it up. As outlined in the last chapter, Return to the Community, it is to develop your consciousness. Love and wisdom come from developing consciousness as we move closer to going home within. It involves contemplation and soulwork until eventually we become torch-bearers, holding a light of hope to all our loved ones and fellow pilgrims.

A Poem for Hope

Between the two worlds there is sunrise and sunset
the time of majestic light and beauty

May the morning light always bring you here
softly, as it lights the world
to bring you back from the other place
the one you make in the dark
that knows you well
and gives you everything

Have you ever felt as though you were on exactly the right path for you? A revelation, a turn of events, an opportunity or an idea emerges and everything in you says "Yes!". This is the way to go. There is a wholehearted commitment right there without having to work out details and pros and cons before knowing it is good for you. It is the right path. I experience it as though a silken thread from my solar plexus, heart and aliveness is spun that pulls me forward into a future with a meaning of great significance, not always logically clear but known in the body-mind. What I do with this beautiful silken thread is a matter of how it is weaved within my consciousness and daily life.

Our silken threads are just like the delicate strands from silkworms. On their own they are fragile and, at first, easily broken. But woven together, they are strong enough to support huge parachutes and weights. They also make beautiful fabrics, a sensory delight to be wrapped in and feel on our skin. We can weave together the personal and collective silken threads of life into something strong and beautiful.

The task is to follow the silken threads that appear in your life.

They appear rarely and could arrive right out of the blue, but there's no denying the silken thread when it is there. It's music, is a calling, a vision, words, sometimes faint, at other times like an Italian opera sung with feeling and gusto, or a breathtaking painting, immediately recognised by the energy, spirit and sense of inner knowing that this is the way for you to go. It resonates through the body-heart-mind, "This is my path forward. I must find a way to do it. This is what I was born to do. It brings everything together. With this, I become whole."

How wondrous and beautiful.

At least, that is the initial reaction. It is full of promise. It dares us to grow and entices us to get on with it and go down this path of life into new territory. As we savour the prospect, the more logical mind kicks in, bringing its many cautions and judgements until it starts to feel like an unpleasantly wet blanket. Self-doubt sets in. We consider all the varieties of risk associated and the possible consequences. The shining path ahead loses its gold as we lose aspiration in favour of doubt: "Maybe I could do this later, when . . . I feel stronger; when I get my next qualification; when I have enough money; when the kids are through school; when I've done more research; when my parents aren't around anymore; when I have a host of supporters; when I'm over this rough patch; when I achieve the top level at work . . ." The list goes on. At best the new path gets postponed indefinitely, at worst the silken thread and its path get dismissed as a bad idea that will never work.

It is easy to break the silken thread when it is new. Simply turn your back, look away or argue against it. Walk off in another direction. Many people never follow their silken threads because it takes them out of their familiar world and it means taking a chance.

I'd like to spend just a little while now having another look at the unlived life, because if it still draws you, it is still a silken thread.

The Unlived Life as a Silken Thread

An unlived life is about the cards we were dealt in combination with choices and decisions we made. First were the circumstances we were born into and the humans who were our parents. We made our way from there all those years ago to this point now, with many people and conditions that helped shape us. We chose to do this and not to do that; to have this career and not that relationship, or the other way around. Sometimes we were taken over by life events, unable to follow the path we wanted to take. How many have spent a life earning a living and never done or known what they loved? Unless we are in a developing world country, we don't always *have* to earn a living the ways set down: we are a living. With some sacrifices, life can be reorganised in a way that we do what matters most. The poet and philosopher Rumi counselled us to be positive about a life that still pulls us:

"Don't grieve. Anything you lose comes around in another form."

We'll explore this further.

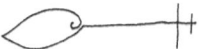

If there is an unlived life you yearn for, and you listen carefully to what that unlived life is telling you—not literally but metaphorically—then you find the task you were born to do. That is the beauty of the unlived life. It is not something forever missed, somewhere in the past. It is our soul still calling us to express our gift, a product of what we are good at and what brings us alive. That is why it is so important not to shut that voice down, even if we first hear it as we are dying. Hopefully, though, we will let in the pure notes of that inner voice earlier.

I've known a number of people to live their unlived life as they were dying. In all cases, it has been a turnaround from being bitter or resentful, domineering or demanding, to be able to accept and give love unconditionally. The strange thing is, that flow of unconditional love is what they really wanted and searched for all their life. It was wonderful they gave and received love at the end, and were filled with grace.

The unlived life is not literal. It is the spirit of it we can express in life now, possibly in ways quite different to our earlier wishing and musings. It doesn't have to be a big vision, although it might be. It simply needs to be connected and alive. For example, Angela dreamed of being singer. She had a good soprano voice, but was never given much chance to develop it beyond school and was left with memories of singing in the choir and a continued longing for making beautiful harmonies in song. In her sixties, her voice was not up to much, but Angela decided she could again create the feeling of being in perfect harmony with others. She found that sense of harmony by joining a group of volunteers working with a wonderful team spirit to help refugees make a new life. What is more, they had a weekend market garden and all sang as they worked, which Angela loved to join in.

The unlived life need not be not in the past. It lies in your future. Because one thing I have seen evidence of over and over: either consciously or unconsciously, we contribute to creating our own future.

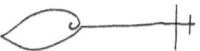

Longing for a life unlived is the soul drawing attention to our personal gift. Rather than take the unlived life as a literal path or a project, regard it as a metaphor. In other words, the specific ideal or project we held so dear is only a vehicle or channel for expressing our gift and soul. It may or may not be grand or clever, but our gift is of our essence and therefore unique and our wonderful and most beautiful value. It is our gold and who we are.

There is a Buddhist story of an enlightened master known in the community only for being a good neighbour who arrived and told stories to the children, grew and shared his veggies, and made villagers laugh and feel valued. After he died the villagers discovered he was the Zen master.

Giving our gift is fulfilment. The unlived life we wish for (possibly a wish for multiple unlived lives) contain the secret of what our gift actually is. It is in the essence, which is the essence of you. There are a multitude of ways we each can embody the unlived life we think we missed and want. If you feel restricted by circumstances, consider the astounding advances and creativity that have come from restriction and scarcity in many fields—writing and arts, science, medicine, research, technology, community, and just finding a path and a strength in the most terrible of life situations. We find ways other than our original life ideal—better ways and reconsider what is the essence of that unlived life. Like the Zen master, our contribution doesn't have to be grand to be of great value and significance, not only to a small community but because they are a microcosm, to the whole. It could be seen that the beauty and strength of the fabric in the whole eminates from the parts, from what we add everyday.

The Dream of Youth

The dream of youth is a silken thread from our long ago past. Many of us had some special fantasy about ourselves during our youth, often around the stage of adolescence. The fantasy, usually secret, might have been about greatness, sexual desirability, fame, heroism or leadership, genius, adventure, artistic brilliance and so on. Although dreams mature with time, the *essence* of the dream of youth contains elements of personal vision and fulfilment, minus the ego urgency. So often in the passage of time and the pragmatics of responsible adulthood the dream is lost, dismantled, forgotten or dismissed as "idealistic", a euphemism for "foolish".

The elements of the dream are seldom applied to *a vision going forward as an adult,* or returned to again in the second half of life. It requires some translation into a mature personal vision as in this story of Ralph.

Not long after he retired from his legal job, his wife died leaving him bereft and desperately lonely. He had become overweight as the years went past, and now spent his days in front of the screen becoming more out of shape. As a youth Ralph aspired to be on the football team. He was stocky, strong, athletic and loved being outdoors. He knew football backwards. But his larger-than-life father had other plans, "Football is for stupid boys, the ones who aren't good at anything else. You'll stick to your studies, Ralph, and make something of yourself. You'll be a lawyer, like your father." Ralph was banned from football practice. All through university, he longed to play and be cheered on as he kicked goals like a hero.

Nearly forty years later here he was, watching football on his big screen. It was a stinking hot day and he decided to buy a beer at half time. Inspired by the athletic footballers, he decided to walk the few blocks to the supermarket instead of drive. On the way, he passed the local park where teenagers were practicing football. Ralph stopped to watch. The guy leaning on the fence beside him had his leg in plaster. They started to chat. He had been the team coach, but injured his leg in a car accident and had to give it up. They were looking for a new coach. "Don't know of anyone do you? It's voluntary. These boys are all at risk—you know, from broken backgrounds. There's no money." Ralph felt a big wave of energy. He gathered his courage. "I used to love playing when I was a kid. It was all I ever wanted to do. Still watch every match to this day. Haven't played for years though." The two men looked at each other a while.

So began a steep learning curve and the best years of Ralph's life.

We may not know exactly where the silken thread is taking us, sometimes it involves big life decisions. Just like the caterpillar has no way of predicting the butterfly will emerge, sometimes we trust there are things we do not yet know, that are magnificent and flourish when allowed to manifest.

There is always a choice. As we age the choice to follow the silken threads is considered more carefully and becomes more an imperative as we face and embody the reality that our own life is finite and we are getting closer to the end than the beginning. We contemplate what to best do with our remaining time and what really matters to us. What will bring us the most heartfelt meaning?

The world's best philosophers and poets tell us about becoming lost, then the long journey to find who we really are. We are each born with something specific to contribute, that emerges from being authentic, knowing self. This has been well-known by the spiritual masters and poets down through the ages. In the thirteenth century, Rumi wrote these marvellous words: "So we come in this world for a particular task, and that is our purpose; if we do not perform it, then we will have done nothing."

The existential philosopher, Martin Buber, put it this way:

"Every person born into the world represents something new, something that never existed before, something original and unique ... If there had been someone like her in the world, there would have been no need for her to be born."

What trace will your actions leave in the world? What echo will your words leave behind? For there will be an echo and a trace you leave behind you, and it can inspire and enrich those who follow. A silken thread always pulls us toward expressing our gift, often in surprising ways that the conscious mind would never dream of. Synchronicity plays a part too as we weave together the strands of silken threads in life and around us.

Calling of the Soul

While we hold and follow our silken thread we can never be lost.

The very essence of it generates our meaning and purpose. It threads and weaves us into the web of life. Let it go and lose the thread, and confusion with lack of meaning easily set in. The silken thread always draws us toward our gift, the particular task that we were born to do. That is our offering and fulfilment, and rarely is it the same as the imprint society stamped on us with the expectations of others. In the long run, pleasing others by living up to their expectations dampens our gift and humbles our innate genius. We are here to give what is innate, not to fit in. It is very simple, as in all of nature: we are growing or we are dying. We contribute or are left. We can all contribute. We all have value and are part of the whole.

Growth, however, involves suffering.

You have experienced a great loss—you can use it to be diminished, to become smaller and begin to die; or you can go on to bring what is inside out, and become a bigger human being. Everyone has the potential for this, can aim for this and claim it. Everyone has a gift to contribute, a task to do, big or small that fulfils us, is good for us and good for others.

Our gift is our vocation. The word "vocation" comes from the Latin *vocationem* with the same Latin root as "voice", meaning a calling, and more precisely, a calling of the soul.

Now you have been through the fire of grieving and the long pilgrimage toward recovery and healing, there are some questions to consider to focus your powers of awareness:

What silken thread is starting to emerge?

What threshold do you stand before now?

This is explored further in the next book, an in-depth look at the two realms of human consciousness, why they exist, and the calling and wonders of developing consciousness. As humans, this is what we are built for. What happens between the two realms of human consciousness is the spiritual meeting place and potential between, and it is here that the weaving together of silken threads occurs to make fabrics of beauty with the strength for living purpose, to prepare our future.

An Invocation

May we come fully into our potential,
our agency, and magnanimity

May the gift that we offer, large or small,
be wholehearted and unconditional

May we reclaim the grace, dignity
and authentic power that our truth bestows

May we each live our life as though it really matters.

IV | Ritual and Contemplation

Practices and Thoughts:
Healing

Ritual and contemplation have proved to be healing and consoling aspects of grief. This is where you can become more active and self-directive in the grief pilgrimage. This section describes a variety of practices to do or contemplate, to accompany passages in Parts I, II and III of the book which outline three stages of grief: loss and ending; the grieving process; then living without your loved-one. Sometimes I go into coaching mode in the practices because when we feel defeated or depleted, defined steps to take are just what is needed. Mostly, though, this is not so much about steps or principles, but invitations to your deeper self to come forward. Contemplation in particular is a way to surface your question, the one that has been with you all along, the question that defines your life and love.

Loss and grief is a chance to know our selves better and understand that others may be suffering too. We can create a place of welcome and shelter, and invite others in.

Rituals are symbolic actions with an intent to create meaning.

Contemplation is free-flowing reflection and investigation of something significant and integral.

Practices tend to be active tasks for expansiveness, development and teaching.

Ritual

Ritual provides an intervening structure. Rituals are symbolic, usually repeated, and often intensify awareness and meaning. An intent is set for the ritual beforehand, with an underlying intent to help us move onto more stable ground internally. Then we have calm and spaciousness for our thoughts and expressions. Grief is powerful and demands our full attention—for some of the time. Giving grief full-time attention over a long period is exhausting and unsustainable. The use of ritual can provide beneficial pacing and rhythm for grieving. Grief must have its say and be allowed full voice; it is too powerful to attempt to bottle up, and rituals are a time grief can be given full expression yet be contained by the simple design of the ritual.

Why do Rituals Work?

Research published in *Scientific American* found that even simple rituals are extremely effective (Gino and Norton). They found rituals performed after losses do alleviate grief. What is more, rituals appear to benefit even people who claim not to believe that rituals work. They cite psychologists who have demonstrated that rituals can have a causal impact on people's thoughts, feelings, and behaviours.

Experiencing the death of a loved-one is a major state of liminality, an in-between time of being at the threshold. There we can gather our self together as we deal with existential concerns we face: their dying, our loss and sorrow and other intense feelings, and the impact on life going forward without our loved-one. Our previous place in the world shifts with their departure. Structured contemplative ritual helps us come to terms with this. A candle ritual, walking meditation, and regular contemplative journal writing are some examples. As we go, our pool of internal resourcefulness are utilised and built up.

One of the most well-known and ancient rituals, also a rite of passage, is known as the vision quest. The aim is to mobilise and focus the particular energy and potential available during a major life transition, coming of age. This is a totally different perspective to the vulnerability, hopelessness or emptiness that is so often feared by those in bereavement, who are also going through major life transition. The grief threshold seems a gloomy place to be because of the magnitude of psychospiritual experience. Yet it is precisely in this state of heightened sensitivity that truths not easily accessed in normal awareness can be brought to consciousness.

Rituals assist in reconnecting our truths and preparing for the vision quest at mid-life, themes explored in the forthcoming book on the two realms of consciousness.

Rites of Passage

A rite of passage is a specific experience that is prolonged over a period of time. It is an initiation requiring self-enquiry. A ritualised liminal experience, it marks an ending and a beginning. Grief is like this. Rites of passage have certain characteristics:

- they amplify a transition
- affect us deeply;
- are an initiation (into grief, into living with loss, into a different life or responsibility)
- call for inner work - as in coming of age, the seeking of wisdom, and grieving
- are developmental, a shift from the small, reactive self to a more expanded, magnanimous self;

- have outcomes such as healing and growth and,
- often involves community support, witnessing, or confirmation.

The Archetypal Pattern

A rite of passage follows the ancient archetypal pattern, simply put as separation, ordeal and return. During separation normal life is interrupted, disrupted and much time is spent alone. There is an awakening of mind and soul, of seeing yourself differently in the world, of insight and sometimes revitalisation like a second birth. This is followed by an ordeal and suffering alone though hardship or menace. Here, you are left to interact instinctively with the world and whatever tests and trials are encountered. This is the liminal work, the transition and grief pilgrimage.

Finally, the ordeal is over and you return to the community in a different and more advanced state. Ideally, your state is confirmed and recognised by the community. You bring a new perspective, your personal gift and energy that has luminosity for a few or many.

Contemplation

To contemplate is to consider deeply and observe attentively. Special conditions help facilitate contemplation, like going to a place (literally or metaphorically) you regard as sacred. The place is sacred because it is consecrated, which I believe you can sanctify yourself with good intent. Furthermore, the place may be a physical setting in nature, in a building, or a certain state of mind. These conditions alone or together are conducive to contemplation.

The purpose of contemplation is basically to discover what is hidden or obscure, and beyond that for me, it is to behold enchantment and wonder.

During contemplation, full and deep consideration is given to something that is on your mind. Uninterrupted, quiet thought with continued attention is called for. Some dictionaries offer meditation and reflection as synonyms to contemplation, although there are differences for example in meditation when the aim is to clear the mind rather than focus a concern or creativity. Contemplation holds the additional and specific practices, intents and associations mentioned, that are not synonymous with meditation but have more similarities with reflection. These practices will likely ring true if you engage in contemplative experience. The evolution of contemplative practice is evidenced in its etymology, so let's take a brief but fascinating look at its origins and associative words.

"Contemplation" comes from the Latin *contemplatus*, meaning "to gaze attentively, observe; consider, contemplate," and originally, "to mark out a space for observation, as an augur (diviner, sage) does". In Latin "contemplation" is made up of the prefix *com* + *templum*. *Templum* is Latin for "temple", originally described as a "piece of ground consecrated for the taking of auguries" (I like that it is "ground" and not a building because ground brings in nature, earth and living plants). "Augur" and "auguries" are from the Old French meaning the "divination from the flight of birds," (how beautiful is that?) "Divination" is from the Old French, meaning "discovering what is hidden or obscure". All this illuminates a fuller meaning of what it is to contemplate which I've put together as:

Comtemplation is to consider deeply on sacred ground and in the temple of your mind-body, to find what has been hidden or obscured.

Contemplation is one of the great wisdom practices found in global and spiritual traditions. A regular practice of contemplation increases awareness and aids insight and transformation. As well as the contemplative aspect, the discipline of regular practice facilitates development. Practice is a repetitive exercise we learn to apply in life from the time we are born; the basics of learning to make word sounds and learning to walk are early examples of practicing a skill or activity. Practice also refers to a regular ritual designed to deepen consciousness, such as a mindfulness or meditation practice.

The most powerful methods of contemplation practice call for the broadening and deepening of consciousness. Contemplative Practice can take the form of free-flowing association, focusing the imagination, the influence of place, immersing yourself in nature, and Contemplative Journalling (a guide to contemplative journalling is available on my website www.dipercy.com).

Practice

Practices are the actions and exercises that accompany or extend contemplation. Practices may refer to rituals as well, but *contemplative practice* differs because it focuses more on exploration, experiment, learning and insights for living. Because practices are carried out in a certain setting—a space made sacred, and at a time conducive to concentration or quieting the mind, that is safe and free of interruption so there is privacy and dedication to the task— you could think of practice as a laboratory of the body-mind-soul.

Contemplative practice is to unearth, discern, or create meaning and growth with enquiry, imagining or experiment to contrast and test fixed notions we have in our mind. Practice is a way to actively aerate suffering and build equanimity and balance.

More broadly, practices are active tasks. They include contemplation, soulwork and journal writing, yoga, walking contemplation, exercises of the imagination, being mindfully in nature, making meaning from dreams, music, texts or poetry. Practices extended to wider life pursuits like mindful teaching, healing, caring, and active dying.

List of Practices

1. Bearing Witness
2. Overwhelm
3. Burnout and Fatigue
4. Self-Care
5. Being the Torch Holder
6. Shielding Contemplation
7. Inner Fire Contemplation
8. Questions for Your Loved-One
9. Happy Community Ritual
10. Grief Mask: A Private Ritual
11. Celebrating Impermanence and Imperfection
12. Free-flowing Ritual
13. Message to Your Loved-One
14. The Person is Gone: Your Relationship Continues
15. Guilt and Grief Contemplation
16. Shame Contemplation
17. Anger and Forgiveness Contemplation
18. Fear Contemplation
19. Entitlement Contemplation
20. A Grounding Meditation
21. The Missed Conversation
22. A Contemplative Journal
23. On Gratitude
24. Self-Forgiveness
25. Letters to Your Self
26. A Lighter Note
27. Giving Back, Generosity and Purpose
28. Harvesting

29. Your Own Death
30. Seeing Beauty Contemplations
31. Seeing Beauty on Waking
32. Silken Thread Meditation

1. Bearing Witness

Bearing witness is not being passive, it is being fully present. On bearing witness to one who is dying, can you give up trying to save them? Can you give up ideas you hold about "a good death"? Can you be with what is without resisting it? Can you trust in what is happening for your loved-one without trying to change it?

Trying to take over and protect our loved-one can blind us to the living experience of the one actively dying. It can obstruct them from taking the lead in their most profound rite of passage. Instead we can minister to them, to witness their dying in their own way.

To do so means crossing the boundary of our own being into a new way of being, one we had never before considered as a part of our life. We are asked to cross the threshold of our own story of living and dying and this can liberate us into a larger vision, a bigger spiritual space with more capacity to bear witness and hold the other in our heart without intruding.

A Practice for Bearing Witness

Remember an experience of your own, one of suffering or fearful apprehension. Bring as much of that experience as you can now into your body and mind. Say out loud or use your journal to recall this experience for five minutes.

Physically change positions so you are seated in a different place, ideally opposite or nearby. Now, as one bearing witness to the experience as it was just told, review what you have said or written for another five minutes. Bring your compassion and equanimity to bear and simply be present as you review. If you want, imagine yourself recalling the experience in the first chair. Be aware of any impulses to solve or save without acting on them. Just remain present.

This is powerful training for simply remaining present and not rushing to save or console the loved-one, but to allow them to express what is arising and really listen and be their witness.

2. Overwhelm

When it all seems too overwhelming, when you just don't know how you're going to get through it, how you can go on, then shorten your timeframe. When you can't think about next month, think about next week. When you can't think about next week, just think about tomorrow. When that seems too much, think about this afternoon; or in two hours time. And when even that is impossible, just go to the next few minutes. For now, you will sit here in this chair for a while. Just stay here. No need to move. After that, maybe you'll have a cup of tea or coffee.

Allow quiet times.

The Healing Power of Nature

Embrace the small moments of grace. Notice them. Whenever you can, go out into nature and, as well as looking at the colours, shapes, textures and movement, listen to the sounds there; feel the wind and sun, feel the trees and the ground you walk on. If you're in the city, look up at the blue sky and clouds, the twilight, or night sky. Marvel at the beauty there.

See life from your soul's view.

When we open our eyes, ears and feel beauty, we become quieter, centred. This is especially so when we are quiet, undistracted and in solitude. Solitudo is Latin for nature. How remarkable is that?

In true solitude, we remember our self as being a part of everything, a part of nature. We rediscover ease, belonging, inspiration and contentment in our own company.

3. Burnout and Fatigue

Sometimes we fail in our intention and commitment. We make mistakes. We can become physically, mentally and emotionally run-down without realising. We are human and vulnerable, like everyone else. A mistake, misunderstanding, or feeling unwell and exhausted is a wake-up call to pay attention to our health, stress levels and wellbeing. It can also be cause for reflection and humility.

Here are some of the facts on burnout from the research by Smith, Segal and Segal for your contemplation and to apply to yourself and others.

What is Burnout?

Burnout is a state of emotional, mental and physical exhaustion caused by prolonged or excessive stress. According to the research by Smith, Segal and Segal, burnout occurs when you feel overwhelmed and struggle to meet constant demands. As the stress continues, you begin to lose the energy and the motivation that led you to take on a certain role or task in the first place.

The term was first used in psychology by Herbert Freudenberger in 1970 and his findings referred to as four progressive stages, summarised here: 1) Idealism and overload, where people show high levels of work enthusiasm and results with engagement to the detriment of self-care. 2) Physical and emotional exhaustion while continuing efforts to cope with symptoms. 3) Dehumaising, trying to protect themselves by distancing and becoming increasingly withdrawn, dominating, antagonistic or controlling while feeling increasingly unhappy. 4) People succumb to despair and intense self-loathing, followed by total withdrawal and breakdown.

As you can see, burnout reduces capacity, self-care, saps energy and interferes with decision making. In 2018 the World Health Organisation described burnout as a new listing in the International Classification of Diseases as characterised by three factors: energy depletion or exhaustion; increased mental distance from the job or negativity and cynicism about the job; and reduced professional efficiency.

Are You At Risk of Burnout?

Anyone who feels the symptoms above including overwork, physical or psychological fatigue, and distancing is at risk of burnout. I have seen a connection to a growing sense of meaninglessness and believing you are undervalued. When caring for someone who is dying, it may be a more demanding role than you ever anticipated and contain a level of responsibility never before encountered. As time goes on, if you give yourself no relief, burnout can mix with feelings of concern and duty. Responsibility becomes a burden and it may seem that no one else is stepping up to help.

Burnout is not only a matter of stress and excessive responsibility. Personality, conflicting responsibilities and lifestyle play a part too. This is truly a time for self-care rather than rising to the demands of past aspirations, such as being the hero, the martyr, the all-giving selfless parent, or the tireless warrior. Read on to 4. Self-Care.

4. Self-Care

There is so much to say about self-care for healthcare professionals and dying companions alike, with much research and advice available. Caregivers often walk a path that leaves no footprints behind except for the beautiful human rapport that occurs between care-giver and 'subject' in the moment. Here is a contribution to alert you to the responsibilities of self-care.

Self Awareness

The central and most important act of burnout prevention and kindness for the self and our loved-one, is our own self awareness. Ignoring and glossing over symptoms of burnout doesn't work (a description of symptoms can be found in 3. Burnout and Fatigue). Like any ill health, symptoms can be healed when attended to early.

Other Self-Care Suggestions

Self-care is actively thinking, planning and acting in ways to prevent burnout, stress and overwhelm. Here are some suggestions:

Find a trusted partner or mentor for support especially during stressful and demanding times. We can be alone in a whole team of professionals or in the midst of the family. Find someone within or outside the workplace or family who is competent and feels safe. That person can support you through painful and demanding situations, remind you that you have limits in respect to your own welfare, and keep watch that you do not unconsciously keep exceeding them.

Support and involve other caregivers.

Make a schedule that is doable and sustainable. Schedule in downtime daily that takes your mind away from death and dying. Allow some time for healthy and refreshing activities you enjoy.

Set limits with your own self-care in mind. Practice meaning "no" or "not right now".

Pay attention to your attitude, the way you are seeing the world and interpreting situations. Watch for growing negativity, anxiety, irritability etc. which indicate signs of stress.

As adults, no one else can self-care for us. Signs of burnout include constant tiredness or exhaustion, increasing cynicism and depression. Signs of stress include sleeplessness, depression and anxiety.

5. Being the Torch Holder

Being the Torch Holder is holding the light of hope. The image is of one holding up a torch to light the way for another (and for yourself) and that is the job of the Torch Holder. It is finding within yourself the will to hold up the light and say some messages of genuine hope and meaning for your loved-one. The hope given must come from your truth.

That does not mean it must be profound or complicated. The simplest things are the most beautiful and hopeful. Sometimes just your presence embodying a belief that your loved-one is safe and will be free is enough.

The idea alone of being the Torch Holder gives you direction when you feel lost or overcome. Know that hope is more powerful than fear and prevails over suffering, powerfully demonstrated by Viktor Frankl in his account of the concentration camps.

The messages you might give are personal and depend on your loved-one's beliefs and acceptance, but be aware these often change close to death and the dying become more accepting and open to beliefs. The best idea I can give you is with this story:

> A daughter who was at a loss as to what to say to her dying father, followed her instinct to sit close and whisper to him. As she stroked his forehead, she whispered sweet messages of her love and all that she hoped for him in death: that he will be enveloped with love, all those he knew and cared for who had passed on will be waiting to greet him, there will be wonder and happiness, he will be forever safe and free, and she will join him when it's her turn to die.

6. Shielding Meditation

As soon as you feel uncomfortable with a person or situation, imagine your protective shield surrounding you.

Take some deep breaths to clear and centre yourself. Visualise a white or warm light wrapping around you, encircling your whole body like an airborne cocoon.

Within this light you are shielded from what is toxic, negative and anything external that can stress you. Much like holy and spiritual teachers are not influenced by toxic words, you too are free of their sting. You hear the words but they no longer harm, leaving you free and unstressed.

To practice, visualise the light wrapped around you, shielding you. Then replay a toxic situation in your mind but this time you are protected by the light and not harmed. Afterwards, dissolve the light knowing you can bring it back at any time.

The more you practice this meditation, the more effective it is in real situations.

A Protective Strategy

A protective strategy is effective when there has been a transgression of your personal boundary. This can feel like verbal or psychological abuse and it can be subtle, but leaves you highly uncomfortable.

When someone is pushing you around, being manipulative, or is unable to self-manage a reservoir of destructive feelings, then you need a strategy to protect yourself. Set limits by drawing a line in the sand and tell them what behaviours are not acceptable and what the consequences will be if repeated. Stay with your side of it. As you do this in your mind, find yourself standing on solid ground within, as May discovered:

> May's dying husband Craig, became more bad tempered and foul mouthed. Walking back into Craig's hospital room, May stood straight. "I will sit with you for a while today, Craig. The minute you start with your foul language and abuse, I'm out that door. Then I may or may not come back

tomorrow.

A simpler strategy is to say, "Stop it" or "No". Both are complete and clear messages requiring no further explanation.

Remember to tell yourself it's all right. You are doing the best you can. Things cannot be perfect.

7. Inner Fire Contemplation

Imagine an inner fire, one that is welcoming and warming. The flame is the passion of what you love—dear people, a love of learning and discovery for instance. It is the willingness to open to life and, with that, to take courage and keep hope.

The quality of inner fire is transformational. It can transform the hardship and obstacles that present.

Illumination

In its illumination
the fire within is life.
In its glow
you come fully alive.
Treasure the moments
of inner life fire.

The Practice:

Where in your body do you locate the fire within?

Take some time to imagine the flame, and bask in its spirit.

Then ask your inner flame 'What is your message?'

Wait for what word, image, feeling emerges.

8. On the Power of Naming Things

Regard this as a personal ritual. Those that love us do not want us to suffer and want us to move on to some fulfilment in life after they have gone. These are questions you have for your loved-one that were not answered. What helps many people in grief is to think about what your loved one would want for you if they were here today; if they were able to talk to you now what would their answer be.

What would they say?

What words of comfort would they give you?

What advice would they give you?

Try forming a question about what is on your mind and then ask it. Actually write it down.

Then answer, in writing, as though you are your loved one writing to you.

To feel released with the blessing of our loved-one, is to be freed to reconnect with life when we are ready. Grief is an expression of love for one lost. It is not meant to be a prison.

9. Happy Community Ritual

In the Japanese Buddhist tradition Bon, is a colourful community ritual when the living commemorate, honour and celebrate the spirits of family members who have died. At Bon festivals, dances that express joy for departed souls are performed in traditional kimonos. The dance takes place around a stage with lit lanterns overhead. The lanterns symbolically serve as beacons to the dead to come and join the celebration. Bon usually takes place during summer months, when it is believed that ancestral spirits return to visit relatives and friends. It is a time of remembrance when families visit and clean gravesites. Food is shared and there are vibrant processions through cemeteries.

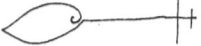

You could hold your own version of "Bon". A happy ritual of family and friends with food, or music and dancing. Ask everyone to bring a happy memory of the departed to share, or some music, a poem or a memento to talk about.

Symbolism linked to meaning will enhance the ritual experience. This is individual to you and your knowledge of the deceased. Make it special with candles (they always give a warming glow), a central fire pit or camp fire if you're in the country. Hold the ritual at a significant time of day, like high noon in cooler months for the advantage of full sun and the illumination of the mind, or at sunset or under the night sky for the gentle connection with wonder and the beauty of living and dying. Perhaps consider asking everyone to wear something of a particular colour, and explain what the significance is in relation to the deceased, or to you in their memory.

10. Grief Mask: A Private Ritual

Many people who are grieving put on a brave face. When at work, out socially or in the community, many present as though everything is all right and they are coping well and getting on with life. The truth may be one of masking their grief. You will have your own understanding of why not appearing personally "together" and controlled is assumed to be socially inappropriate. No wonder grief is such a lonely process with such high expectations. What a burden would be lifted if we felt free to share the emotions that accompany loss and endings.

I heard of a lovely idea. It is to turn masking grief into a real grief mask—rather than a mask that disguises how you feel, one that expresses how you really feel (or two masks, one of each). Unless you choose otherwise, this grief mask is for your eyes only so you can be free in your expression and not concerned about whether it's pretty basic artistically.

The Practice

Draw or paint a grief mask that represents how you really feel, using all the colour and drama that you can muster. To go all out, make a 3D version in clay or paper mache (instructions are on the internet). It is a way to express deep feelings of grief and surface inner resources like compassion and balance. To express rather than repress feelings of grief is to release them.

You might like to note your comments and insights. Do another grief mask later on, in three months, then six months, then twelve. Over time, it gives you a record of your grieving journey, the stages you go in to and out of, and the eventual lifting of suffering.

11. Celebrating Impermanence and Imperfection

We can take a leaf from the book of Japanese philosophy. Wabi-sabi is the appreciation of the beauty in imperfection. Imperfection arises from the natural law of impermanence and the the natural progression of the ageing of things such as rusting, the silvering of timber, the cragginess of old trees, and the natural ageing of human beings.

In Japan, evidence of ageing is even highlighted like the fine cracks in an old cup or piece of pottery that come with age, regarded as adding to its beauty, are enhanced by rubbing gold dust into them to emphasise the age and bring out the fine cracks. The lines on faces and bodies tell the story of that persons life, to be respected and revered as a reservoir of wisdom. Wabi-sabi celebrates impermanence and seeing the beauty and aesthetics in imperfection.

Go ahead. Celebrate your own and your loved-one's imperfection and Wabi-sabi.

The Practice

Write a list of your loved-one's imperfections. Beside each one write or draw a symbol for the aesthetic, appreciation or love you have of that imperfection, and as a reflection of their life experience.

Try doing the same for your self.

12. A Free-Flowing Ritual

You might want to leave this ritual quite unstructured and open-ended, and do what seems right at the time. If that is crying all the way through, it's all right. This is your ritual and your space for whatever you need, alone or with invited others.

You might decide to play your loved-one's favourite music.

Or to look at photos and relive your shared life together.

Or to be immersed in warm water in the bath if that is what is called for.

To make it a ritual, mark it with the symbols of the ritual: a beginning, a symbolic meaning, and the ritual ending.

13. The Message

There may be times you want to say something particular that has been on your mind, perhaps something special to your loved-one who has died. A ritual is a good place to do it. Set up the place for the ritual and your intent, so you can:

Reflect and silently think through your message to your loved-one (this is the most difficult as it's hard to stay focused);

Say or sing your message out loud; or

Write your message out as a special note. Think about ceremoniously burning or burying your note with a wish for your message, or tearing it into tiny pieces and releasing it to the wind. I've found writing then releasing or burning the note to be calming and symbolic of letting go with love and a beautiful sadness.

14. The Person is Gone: Your Relationship Continues

This is a message of healing. Your relationship continues internally, in what goes on in within you, heart and mind. This is your time now. You no longer are the dying companion. You are freed from the responsibilities of being the carer or bearing witness. That time has passed.

Many emotions come up with surprising intensity during grief. Now is not the time to be harsh with yourself, to scold yourself or be the severe judge. Our rational selves can be put to better use by extending protection and kindness to aid and guide us through this liminal time.

When your relationship with the dying person was coloured by their anger and a bitterness that wounded you, forgiveness can seem hard or inappropriate. Sometimes it is not so much we forgive their actions that harmed, but we are able to step back to a bigger perspective of our loved-one's life and experiences that were beyond their control that impacted and shaped their. With that perspective, we can acknowledge and respect that life can be indiscriminately harsh and wounding, leaving lasting damage.

In humility for all who are living and dying, we pay tribute that all humans do the best they know how.

As in a pilgrimage, sometimes what we encounter in the grief passage surprises us. The following five practices and emotions of grief, shame, anger, fear and entitlement, are some of the surprising upsurges that sometimes surface during grief. They are presented to you for contemplation and to start the healing.

15. Guilt and Grief Contemplation

Mistakes will be made and sometimes we fail in our intention and commitment to be present and loving. We can physically run-down, psychologically burn-out and not attend properly to our health. We are human and vulnerable, like everyone else. During grief, a mistake or misunderstanding with a good friend can be a wake-up call to pay attention to our health and wellbeing. It can also cause self-blame and relentless rumination. A mistake, argument or failure with your dead loved-one can trigger relentless guilt.

"If only I had done this and not done that."

"What if I had seen it coming and took the right action sooner?"

"Why couldn't I love them more?"

Questions like this can plague people and become the centre-point of grief, going over and over the same ground in the mind without rest. Ongoing guilt is crippling. It is a universal human experience that makes the spirit sink and depletes confidence. At the heart of guilt is having betrayed someone to something. Why is it some humans carry a lot of guilt and a big conscience while others are not bothered by the same thing? Guilt in grief has little respite or forgiveness except coming to a place of forgiving our self. Existential guilt is born from childhood experiences. In childhood we acquire certain social norms, we are taught to do some things that are good and not to do others that are bad and suffer consequences like physical or psychological punishment if we don't comply. Causing someone to feel guilt is well-known as a psychological instrument of control.

Two Kinds of Guilt

The truth is there are two kinds of guilt. One is a failure to meet the expectations and standards of others. We feel guilty for disappointing or offending them, failing to gain their approval and do what they want, feeling we've failed to deliver what they need, we have hurt them, or been unable to be sufficient in what was needed.

The other kind of guilt is a result of betraying the self and going against our true nature. Many stories illustrate this and this one was tragic, told to me by a lawyer not long before he died.

> I have run out of time. I've become an old man. All I really wanted was to walk free in the world, live amongst nature in a simple country life and grow vegetables, fruit and native plants. Instead, I spent my life in the law dealing with criminals and the ugly side of life. It was expected I would follow in my father's footsteps and because I thought that was what I must do, that is what I did. I lived my life for them, not for myself. All I have to show for it is mediocrity and unfulfilment. Suddenly, it's too late and soon I'll be gone. It's against my principles to complain, but I feel such sadness. I have no hope left. By trying to make others happy, I've betrayed myself."

To know if we have betrayed our self, our soul, we need to know who we are, who the self is, to know our soul and our truth. Sometimes it is called retrieving the soul. Once we know our soul, once we can hear it speak and sing, then our spirit soars. See Chapter 15, Silken Threads.

16. Shame Contemplation

Shame and guilt are close. Both are painful, crushing emotions that can rise up as part of grief. Guilt is summarised as "there's something wrong with what I did", whereas shame is about "there's something wrong with me". We feel shame and condemn our self. It is a heavy burden to carry.

Grief is sorrow and sadness, deep intimacy and beautiful in its unique way. But for those taught to tranquillise or hide soft feelings, grief can become grim and cruel. Ignoring these feelings doesn't work because although they are soft, make no mistake they are powerful. They spill out in unintended ways and can transform into "strong" feelings like anger. Emotions do not stay silenced for ever and erupt when they have festered and gathered enough energy and are acted out. In hindsight, that leads to shame as the over-reaction is realised, thus creating another level of suffering on top of grief. In addition, when we have learned to deaden certain emotions, the consequences are that all emotions are deadened, including the capacity for joy and love.

Shame heals by being acknowledged, owned and expressed. It means being willing to say plain words like, "I feel shame"; "I regret"; or "I feel responsible and heartbroken now." Say the words with someone you trust and talk about the emotion together, how it has affected both of you in life and, if you want, what particular happened. There is no shame in this admission, if it is shared with genuine humility as part of being imperfect and recognising false assumptions operating at the time. Seek forgiveness. Forgive your self.

17. Anger and Forgiveness Contemplation

Sometimes there is anger. Anger can be part of grieving. Not always, but sometimes. Feeling angry doesn't mean being bad or twisted. If you are not normally an angry person, it is more likely pent up emotion being released. On losing her life partner, one woman said she was astonished at the course her grief took. She expected to feel great sorrow but she felt rage, and it wasn't a passing emotion but went on for months. Her rage lessened when she was alone and after a while she worked that out she could spend most of her time in solitude where she felt better. Later on she talked about her unexplained rage with close friends and family, saying she was truly sorry for offence she caused.

Anger plays tricks. There is a distinction between experiencing anger and acting on it. Anger is tricky because we convince ourselves we are in the right, others are not, and collect evidence to support it. Anger and resentment can be a delayed reaction to our loved-one's mistreatment of us as they were dying, or surface from a previous time in the relationship or come from way back in our own life. Whatever the stimulus, nothing constructive comes from keeping anger alight and burning. A choice is available: keep fuelling the anger or forgive.

Why keep anger going when we source better energy from other emotions that don't cost us as much?

Emotions come and go like waves of the sea and are always in motion (e-motion). We can step back and be more aware of the tides of emotion as they wash up within and be the observer of our emotions rather than the one who acts on them. Acting on anger perpetuates it and must always have a justification, a story of defence and righteousness. Therefore, that is what we do in anger, weld together the pieces in a way to justify our anger and position. Anger is dangerous in this way because it is self-righteous.

It can happen the other way around. The one dying can become angry and harsh so that those closest are left hurt and wounded. No matter what our loved-one said to us, we are responsible for our emotions. Someone hurts us and we can carry that hurt for years, even for the rest of life. Better to take the wounding no matter how deep it goes, take time to bathe it in care and healing, then piece together the learning and understanding sufficiently to forgive and let it go.

When anger or hurt arises from past events with a deceased loved-one, which may or may not be about them directly, we are best to acknowledge it. After the internal burning subsides enough to give us breathing space, we can start our enquiry, our soulwork, an internal enquiry that holds no prisoners. We seek truth. We look into our own participation in the matter from start to finish. We look out for what it can teach us and what to forgive.

18. Fear Contemplation

Not everyone feels fear during grief, but for those who do, it can be more worrying than the fearsome thing itself. We can be afraid of grief . Because fear can be a hidden side of bereavement, we may judge ourselves weak or crazy if we get scared. We can feel fear for many reasons, both practical and psychological.

Fear is Intelligent

When fear gets us out of immediate and real danger, it is intelligent. Fear itself serves an essential purpose, it alerts us to danger and gets us ready for action. When the immediate danger subsides, so does the fear. Danger includes real threat to our life and safety. When someone dies and we have depended on them psychologically, emotionally and/or practically, their death is felt as a threat. We either need to look for a replacement or we need to grow. No matter what your circumstances, I fully encourage you to grow.

When fear lingers on past the danger period, it closes us down. Thoughts become negative and suspicious. Thoughts can blame others, even our most trusted, and fearful thoughts of scarcity and lack start to predominate, of not having enough to go around. It may be the toughest time of life, but negative and scarcity thinking escalate and compound anxieties and stress, when what we need is the just the opposite. To be calm.

Sometimes fear is not straightforward. It can take some strange twists and turns. We laugh at Woody Allen's paranoia about dying that resonates with us, "I'm not afraid of dying. I just don't want to be there when it happens."

There is the fear of fear. That is not straightforward fear. How do you know if it is fear of fear? You might already have an inkling; it is when fear lingers on and on, and becomes non-specific, attached to many things. So ask yourself this question: Is being afraid, being in a state of ongoing fear, one of the worst things I can imagine? If "Yes" comes pretty easily, there's your answer. Fear of fear is when we are like the Man of La Mancha, tilting at windmills, which is about as productive as trying to fight or flee from our own shadow.

Buddhist psychology and existential therapies teach that whatever dominates our thoughts becomes our reality, our existence. To notice and identify this is the first step in changing it.

Therefore, notice your thoughts. Write out your fears. Enquire into where they have come from, and trace back to what started them—and I mean way back, into our personal history, and our roots, like what made our parents afraid, and before them our ancestors.

I recommend using a special notebook as a Contemplation Journal (also see A Grounding Meditation).

19. Entitlement Contemplation

Grief changes people, especially where money is concerned. The deceased's will and estate can be explosive. For those unable to contain their indignation or grasping urges, it erupts like a volcano. Justified by entitlement thinking, "I deserve this, it is owed to me" they are blind and deaf to anything to the contrary. It is as though their very survival depends on it, which is just where we are taken back to psychologically, to survival instinct. And just in case you think you are above all that, we can all get caught up in this sort of entitlement and expectation. Below is an example followed by a way to understand what is going on.

The one closest to the deceased is preoccupied with grief and may have to deal with the funeral as well, leaving the door open for others to act on their own expectations. Opportunism can come out to take advantage of those who are more vulnerable, as in this story.

> Even before the old lady died, the two of them were in her home, going through her belongings and everything of value, deciding what they would claim as their own, because after all they deserved it. Then unannounced, they put their list to her widower. They had it all worked out and their demands confused him; he was still in shock and coming to terms with the demise of his lifelong partner. They went through the items on their list, "We'll take this, you can have that. We can have all our things packed up and clean out of your way as soon you agree, so it's one less area to worry about." Befuddled, he agreed, believing these two were his trusted allies and after all they were family and would be fair. He supposed it was his own thinking that was woolly and saw it weighted their way. They were young and clear headed. They knew best right now and would look after him.

What causes people, normally nice enough, to become grasping? To put it down to greed doesn't satisfy because what lies underneath greed.

I believe it is those who fear scarcity, who harbour an existential and uninvestigated fear about their survival. When grasping and accumulation is the typical coping mechanism, inner resources have not been developed to deal with their own vulnerability.

If you have to deal with others who become grasping about money and material things, take time to consider the options they put to you in this light. It is helpful to think about their motives in this way, and try understanding their fear, approach them with some compassion, and not to be pressured to agree to anything quickly nor without due consideration from your relevant professional supporters.

Ask these questions of yourself also.

20. A Grounding Meditation

For times of loneliness, anxiety, or just feeling out of rhythm with yourself.

It helps to feel grounded. We can literally re-ground our self using our physical body. Here are some guidelines:

If you have some garden available, go there, or go out to a park, a beach, or somewhere that is special. Otherwise, find a quiet place inside where you feel safe and will not be interrupted. If appropriate, ask others not to disturb you.

Take off your shoes and stand barefoot on the ground, feet shoulder-width apart.

Breathe deeply.

Close or half-shut your eyes and know you are perfectly balanced. Focus on the sensation of the soles of your feet on the ground.

Wiggle your toes into the dirt as though you are gripping the earth.

As you do so, know that you are getting a grip in multiple ways.

Feel the effect of gravity on your body, keeping you safe and firmly in place. Take more deep breaths, slowly.

Say some affirmations to yourself such as, "I am grounded. I am balanced. I have a grip on my life. I am safe. I can let go of my fear. I choose hope."

Be aware that you are more centred. You can become more and

more centred every day.

Feel the air and other elements on your face. Enjoy the luxury of being alive.

21. The Missed Conversation

If you did not have any conversations, or too few of them about what your life would be after your loved-one has gone, whether they were a parent, friend, guru or life-partner, you can have the conversation now that they have died, irrespective of whether you believe in life after death.

You know them well enough . . .

What would they say to you?

Coming from a position of love and being released from worldly troubles, what would they say now?

What would they want for you? What advice would they give? What words of comfort?

When you're alone and without interruption, have the conversation as though they are there in the room with you. Reply to yourself as though you are your loved-one. Keep it going: reply and response. See what happens. Another option is to journal the conversation as though you have it with your loved-one.

When you do this, **talk to your loved-ones best self**, not a version of them that was frightened, angry or in pain. Talk to the one you know was their truth.

22. A Contemplative Journal

For your contemplative journal, chose a special book whenever you can, one you like aesthetically to look at and feel the pages, so that is a pleasure to write in.

Keeping a diary, stream of consciousness notes, and contemplative journalling are all different in characteristics and purpose.

Diaries primarily record events, facts, dates and other information.

Stream of consciousness writing is the expression and clearing of thoughts, emotions and worries as they arise in the mind; this can be negative or positive, connected or unrelated, trivial or significant, resentful or loving, confused or clear, and it has an essential cleaning purpose that is important especially at times of uncertainty and turmoil. I have used it as a way of starting the day and clearing out my mind, almost every day, for the past forty years.

A Contemplative Journal is a way of focusing contemplation, that is, "To consider deeply on sacred ground and in the temple of your mind-body, to find what has been hidden or obscured." (See the introduction to Contemplation at the start of Part IV.) The following practices provide suggestion for the content to explore.

23. On Gratitude

Journal writing is perfect for contemplating gratitude toward someone, either in the form of narrative about them or a letter to them. Gratitude is a form of beauty in action, it encourages us to see others from our soul.

> Note down all you are grateful for that your loved-one brought into your life. Describe specifically what it meant to you, how it helped, made you feel, opened your eyes, brought you awareness, etc.

> Write down what you returned to your loved-one and the affect

on you of having them receive your gift or response.

Note all you value and love about them, including faults or bad jokes that you also find endearing.

Describe any moments of grace with your loved-one or brought about by them.

24. Self-Forgiveness

We make mistakes and choices that cause all sorts of wounding to others, and directly or by association to our selves as well. Without forgiveness and healing, they can stay in the back of the mind for life and we berate ourselves, feel the weight of guilt and suffering long after the event, interfering with life, relationships and the future. Here are some steps to self-forgiveness.

Recharge.

To begin forgiveness, first let go the event or mistake and allow your regret to rest for a while. Park it. Leave the memory alone and detach from it. Do something involving: embark on a project, meditate or do yoga every day, go for long walks in a forest or by a river, visit art galleries, meet old friends, clean up or do those house repairs you've been putting off. Activities give you a rest from the memory, a chance to recharge. If the weight of the memory is too much, go to the next step.

Resist punishment.

Hold back. Desist. Nip all punitive thoughts in the bud (toward your self and others). The more you indulge in punishing thoughts, the more these thoughts multiply and the more punitive your actions become. It is harsh on you and harsh on others if you blame them.

Refuse to wallow.

Don't continue to dwell or keep the event or "if only wish" in the centre of mind by going over and over it. Let making it fade your intention.

Release yourself.

Surrender to forgiveness. Release others if they are involved. Decide that the suffering and punishment already experienced is the debt paid in full. You are free of bad feeling from now on. No further payment is required. If it's helpful, issue a pardon stating full wholehearted forgiveness and release.

Set up a ritual of self-forgiveness.

Have an image or moment of the event or time the transgression occurred and formally say you are released from it and forgiven. During the ritual, dispose of the image or bless the mementoes if you must keep it.

25. Letters to Your Self

Writing letters brings out the undiscovered and innately wise parts of our selves and gives voice to them on the page. We underestimate how much living we have done and the deep insight and range of experience we hold within our bodies and memory banks. Letters to our self can surprise, comfort and counsel. Either start the letter with a specific intent (such as affirmations, forgiveness, healing, a reminder of humour), and then see what emerges and what you would most like to read in the future. Alternatively, try writing as though you are your ancestors giving loving advice.

> **Write a letter to yourself to be opened and read in 3 months' time.**
>
> **Write a letter to yourself to be opened and read one year from now.**
>
> **Write a letter from one or more of your ancestors speaking to you with wisdom and love,** to be opened on a day in the future that has significance for you, such as January 1, your birthday, mid-winter, an anniversary.

26. A Lighter Note

To be able to smile, to laugh again and feel the lightness of being once more are wonderful moments. It has taken me a long time, I would say two years to feel a sense of full enjoyment and glee, but then I'm probably slower than most.

So I include these on a lighter note, and I mention them because it makes me laugh everytime I think of them.

In pursuit of endearing options for keeping the loved-one close after passing on, I heard this rather bizarre course of action from the United States from an enthusiastic innovation company. There is a trend to have the body freeze dried. From there it can be broken down into tiny pieces and remoulded into creative alternatives: a birdbath for your garden or what have you.

Woody Allen captures some universal fears about dying through revealing his own. Asked about what legacy he wants to leave when he dies he said, "I don't want to achieve immortality through my work. I want to achieve it through not dying."

Woody Allen doesn't believe in an afterlife, however, he says, "I'm bringing a change of underwear. Just in case."

27. Giving Back, Generosity and Purpose

Returning to the community or to particular others, gives us a sense of purpose. The two go together—do something for others that is needed, or helpful or just plain kind, starts to develop a purpose and enhances generosity and kindness. Our purpose can be humble and local, or grand and global as long as it engages the soul, and when it does so, it contributes to humankind. The way I understand it, life purpose is not one of self-importance but one to aid others and life as a generous and noble part of humanity. Here are research findings on the individual benefits of giving back, generosity and personal purpose:

Neuroscientist Dr Richard Davidson has a profusion of data showing that when individuals engage in generous and altruistic behavior, they actually activate circuits in the brain that are key to fostering well-being.

People with a sense of purpose were half as likely to develop Alzheimer disease after seven years, according to research of neuropsychologist Patricia Boyle et al., at JAMA Psychiatry

Cardiologist Randy Cohen conducted a large meta-analysis at Mt Sanai Hospital, and found that a high sense of purpose correlates with a 23 percent reduction in death from all causes.

A meta-analysis by Morris Okun et al found volunteering reduces the risk of death by 24 percent.

What thoughts does this raise for you?

Can you imagine something to look forward to and start during in the next year?

28. Harvesting

You could try this idea, originally from a generous and smart man named Matt Church, intended for thought leaders to advance themselves and their work, but it translates beautifully to the context of grieving.

Each year find a single word to use as a guide for the year, a word that that represents your direction in life and what lights you up. Your word could represent something you want to do or be.

It can be a word applied to part of your life you want to grow, that is a special aspiration you hold, a word that will lead to action and doing something. This is important for grief pilgrims who are still sensitive to the world, open to others' needs and may have had new insights along their way through the dying time and grief following. At this point, life starts to take on new meaning in many ways and especially in what really matters. Let your word for the year symbolise what you truly aspire to and use it to keep focus and stay motivated.

Regardless of your age, your word is about being, rather than doing, about an eminent quality or state of mind you want to nurture. My word for this year is "Harvest". I keep it in mind to remind me I am harvesting my life now at my life-stage, and to keep me on track and learning so I can produce good harvests. My word reminds me to stay healthy and vital to keep harvesting for the next few decades.

Over the last two years of grieving I've reflected on the mystery of dying and that each year my death comes closer. That makes me want to get on with harvesting, to do what I was born to do, and be who I was born to be with all the gusto, love and vitality that I have to give.

Once you have your word, write it down and put it where you will see it. And I mean really see it.

29. Your Own Death

For years now I've been practising my own death. This is in the hope it will be like an ascension, that no matter what physical shape I am in, my spirit will soar amongst the beautiful twilight stars and I will be filled with love and peace. The moment of dying will be the ultimate moment of living. I have no idea if it will work but I'm moving along with great hope. If it turns out to be entirely different and I fight death like a warrior banshee, well so be it. The main thing is I am not afraid. Hope is powerful.

My theory is that when we practice and rehearse anything, we build inner resources to assist with the reality and create a good expectation. To start contemplating our own dying and death long before it happens means we start facing and dealing with our fears and resistances now, rather than having them descend on us all together right at the end.

Here is a gentle visualisation to repeat as a way to strengthen a loving and peaceful attitude to dying.

Decide your best attitude to death and set it as the intent.

With eyes closed or half closed, imagine you are dying. See the person or people you most want to have by your side, or alone if that is your preference.

Know that you accept and appreciate your whole life, the good and the bad, and be filled with gratitude for all that living has brought you.

Know that you are releasing the smaller, earthly self into the infinite stream of being.

Imagine being filled with wonder, fine scents, lightness and love as you let go and surrender into peace and beauty.

When you open your eyes, rest for a while in love and grace.

If we are fortunate we will be aware of our death and no matter what the circumstances, it will be more beautiful than we can imagine.

30. Seeing Beauty Contemplations

Beauty is powerfully transformative. When we see beauty around us it uplifts the spirit. Children do this naturally. I recommend the following meditation is done in a garden or park if possible, but I have also discovered a world of wonder by gazing up close at a small bunch of herbs and lawn daisies. On another occasion doing this meditation, I remembered a treasured childhood book I had not thought of in sixty years and was again filled with the beauty and enchantment of its words and paintings.

Start by taking some deep belly breaths and relaxing your body. When you are ready, remember or imagine being three or four or five years old. Can you recall what it was like? Do you have an image of yourself around that age? How were you dressed, what did you look like, what games did you like to play?

Does a certain time of year come to mind? What sounds do you remember? Often we recall particular smells associated with a childhood time.

Now instead of looking at yourself, see if you can remember some of the excitement, curiosity and magic of childhood. Look through the eyes of your three or four or five year old self, eyes open to receive the world; eyes pure, clear, full of wonder and fascination.

31. Seeing Beauty On Waking

On waking each morning, make sure there is something you love or find beautiful to open your eyes to. A flower, a sprig of fragrant pine, a lovely image, a piece of special music, or a garment of clothing. Whatever is beautiful to you. When you place it in your room the previous night, do so from the heart, setting the intent of beauty.

Throughout the day, recalling that beautiful image is like returning home. When you face the difficulties of the day like meeting others who are stressed and don't treat you well, or you may not treat others well yourself, in your mind return home to your symbol of beauty. Rest there for a moment. Feel your breathing. Know that seeing beauty is replenishing your soul. No matter what goes on in the external world, know you can always create these small moments of grace.

32. Silken Thread Meditation

With feet
firmly on the earth . . .
Breathe.
Centre your body
freshen your mind . . .

Imagine a silken thread
soft and strong rising
from deep down
up through your body . . .
See it engaging
lighting up
your 7 chakras in turn
the root chakra base of the spine
the lower belly sacral chakra . . .
solar plexus . . .
the heart . . .
the throat . . .
the third eye . . .
up to the crown . . .
the silken thread runs on
up higher and higher
to the beauty of twilight
weaving a silken cloth
with all the energy
and wonder
of the universe

Bibliography

Albom, M., (2015), Tuesdays With Morrie, Sattva Publications

Bohm, D. (1980), Wholeness and the Implicate Order, Routledge & Kegan Paul

Bradatan, C., (2015), Dying for Ideas: The Dangerous Lives of the Philosophers, Bloomsbury Academic

Buber, M., (1970), I and Thou, Charles Scribner's Sons

Campbell, J., (1993), Hero with A Thousand Faces, Fontana

Castaneda, C., (1974), Tales of Power, Touchstone

Chopra, D. (2016), Quantum Healing, Bantam Books

Clifford, K., Who Cares for the Carers? Literature Review of Compassion Fatigue and Burnout in Military Health Professionals, JMVH Review Article, Vol. 22, No. 3

Csikszentmihalyi, M. (2016), Flow and the Foundations of Positive Psychology, Springer Netherlands

Dali Lama, Tutu, D., (2016), The Book of Joy, Penguin Random House, UK

Dante, Alighieri, The Divine Comedy, Longfellow, H.W., translator, Labyrinth

Davidson, R., (2015), The Human Brain Deconstructing Mindfulness, Talk given at Davos World Economic Forum

Davidson, R., (2015), YouTube talk https://www.youtube.com/watch?v=EPGJU7W0N0I

Doidge N., (2015) The Brain's Way of Healing: Stories of Remarkable Recoveries and Discoveries, Bolinda Publishing

Drury, C., Hunter, J., (2016), The Hole in Holistic Patient Care, Open Journal of Nursing, Vol.6 No.9

Dweck, C., (2007), Mindset: The New Psychology of Success, Ballantine Books

Eckhart, E., (1909), The Book of Divine Consolation, Translated from the Italian by M.G.Steegman, Chatto and Windus, London, New York

Frankl, V., (1959), Man's Search for Meaning, Boston: Beacon Press

Gino, F, Norton, M.I., (2013), Why Rituals Work, Scientific American

Herman, C.P. (2001), Spiritual needs of dying patients: a qualitative study, Oncology Nursing Forum, Jan-Feb;28:67-72.

Jung, C.G., (1967), Memories, Dreams and Reflections, Harper Collins

Jung, C.G., (1968), The Collected Works of C. G. Jung, Volume 12 Psychology and Alchemy, Routledge.

Kornfield, J., 2008, The Wise Heart, Rider.

Marshall, E., Marshall, M., (2020), Wellbeing Through Meaning: burnout prevention for the helping professions, Ottowa Institute of Logotherapy

Maslow, A. (1962), Toward a Psychology of Being, Viking Press

Merton, T.J., (1985), Disputed Questions, Harvest edition

Merton, T.J., (2014), Thoughts in Solitude, Franciscan Media

Mills, B. and Sparks, N, (1990), Wokini, Hay House Inc

O'Donohue, J., (1997), Anam Cara, Bantam Books

Percy, D.E., 2017, The New Elders, Practicing the Wisdom Arts, unpublished manuscript

Pink, D., (2009), Drive: The Surprising Truth About What Motivates Us, Canongate

Plato, (2008), The Symposium, Cambridge University Press

Rumi, (1997), The Essential Rumi, HarperCollins

Seligman, M, (2011), Flourish: A New Understanding of Happiness and Wellbeing, Nicholas Brealey Publishing

Smith M., Segal J., Segal, R., (2015), Preventing Burnout,

Snyder, G., (2015), This Present Moment, Publishers Group West

Sogyal Rinpoche, (1992), The Tibetan Book of Living and Dying, HarperCollins

Yalom, I. D., (2008), Staring at the Sun, Jossey-Bass

About the Author

I want to engage readers in their capacity for transcendence, of seeing the world just differently enough to realise there is an ascent following every descent. It seems to be the polarity of life, yet it is a continuum and a healing cycle. The descent into suffering cannot be avoided, but once fully experienced, you are free to rise up and take flight. Once again, you see the beauty in the world, hear the song sung for you and know how beautiful and resilient you are.

Diana Percy, writer, poet, counsellor, has conducted a board advisory and executive mentoring business for 35 years. She is founder of Organisation Development Australia, and taught psychodynamics to post-graduates at Royal Melbourne Institute of Technology University; trained crisis and grief counsellors in psychiatric services; served as guest faculty with the Gestalt Institute of Melbourne; led 30-day immersions to remote desert regions for artists; and started her career as a counsellor and group therapist. Diana is an Australian and Irish citizen living in Melbourne, Australia.

www.dipercy.com

books@dipercy.com

www.ingramcontent.com/pod-product-compliance
Lightning Source LLC
Chambersburg PA
CBHW021431080526
44588CB00009B/494